HOW TO RAISE
YOUR MAN

ROSE DeWOLF

HOW TO RAISE YOUR MAN

THE PROBLEMS OF A NEW STYLE WOMAN IN LOVE WITH AN OLD STYLE MAN

FRANKLIN WATTS | 1983
NEW YORK | LONDON | TORONTO | SYDNEY

Library of Congress Cataloging in Publication Data
DeWolf, Rose.
How to raise your man.
1. Husbands. 2. Wives. 3. Equality.
4. Interpersonal communication. I. Title.
HQ756.D48 1983   646.7'8   83-10175
ISBN 0-531-09808-7

Copyright © 1983 by Rose DeWolf
All rights reserved
Printed in the United States of America
6 5 4 3 2 1

CONTENTS

INTRODUCTION
1

CHAPTER 1
THESE ARE THE TIMES
THAT TRY WOMEN'S SOULS
5

CHAPTER 2
GIVING A MIRACLE A CHANCE TO HAPPEN
19

CHAPTER 3
NEW STYLE, OLD STYLE
37

CHAPTER 4
THE NEW GUILT
51

CHAPTER 5
WHO WAS THAT MASKED MAN?
61

CHAPTER 6
MAKING THINGS WORSE THAN THEY ARE
73

CHAPTER 7
GETTING HIS ATTENTION
79

CHAPTER 8
THE GARY COOPER SYNDROME
91

CHAPTER 9
GOING THROUGH NAGGING WITHDRAWAL
103

CHAPTER 10
TWO CAN SWEEP AS NEATLY AS ONE
119

CHAPTER 11
WORKING IT OUT
133

CHAPTER 12
GETTING A SECOND OPINION
143

CHAPTER 13
THERE ARE LIMITS
155

ACKNOWLEDGMENTS

A few words about those who helped me with this book. . . .
 Actually I'd like to say more than a few words about that little band whose inspiration, encouragement, and enthusiasm got me going and kept me going on this book. Specifically: my literary agents, Arthur and Richard Pine; my editor, Liz Hock; my friend, Julie Liedman; and (of course) my husband, Bernard Ingster. I'd like to say thank you at least a few million times, but for reasons of space and printing costs I'll just have to let one big thank you stand for them all.
 I'd also like to list here the name of each and every friend who made a contribution along the way. But I won't. Frankly, I'm afraid I'd mistakenly leave out someone who would love to be mentioned, or mistakenly mention somebody whose identity I promised to disguise by using a fake first name. But I do thank them.
 Finally, for the further information of the reader, as well as in appreciation, I provide the following professional identifications of those experts in male-female relationships most often quoted in the book:
 Dr. Aaron Beck is professor of psychiatry at the University of Pennsylvania and director of the Center for Cognitive Therapy; Dr. Walter Brackelmanns appears in the TV series "Couples" and has a private psychiatric practice

in Encino, California; Dr. Naomi Dank is executive director of the Montgomery County Emergency Service in Norristown, Pennsylvania; Mary Davenport is on the staff of the Center for Adult Development in Philadelphia and has a private marital therapy practice; Dr. Norman Epstein is assistant professor of psychology in psychiatry at the University of Pennsylvania and director of research of the Center for Cognitive Therapy; Dr. Lillian Glass is assistant professor of communications arts and sciences at the University of California at Berkeley; Sally Green is a marriage and family counselor with the Marriage Council of Philadelphia; Lynn Hubschmann is director of social services at Pennsylvania Hospital; Lynn McMahon is executive director of Women in Transition in Philadelphia; Dr. David Reed is associate professor of psychiatry and human behavior at Jefferson Medical College and has a private marriage and family therapy practice in Bryn Mawr, Pennsylvania; Dr. Clifford J. Sager is clinical professor of psychiatry at Mount Sinai School of Medicine, New York City, and author of *Marriage Contracts and Couples Therapy* (New York: Brunner/Mazel, 1976); Dr. John Scanzoni is professor of family relations at the University of North Carolina at Greensboro, a member of the Family Research Center, and the author of *Sex Roles, Women's Work and Marital Conflict* (Lexington, Mass.: Lexington Books, 1978) and, with Dr. Maximiliane Szinovacz, professor of sociology at Florida State University at Tallahassee, of *Family Decision-making* (Beverly Hills: Sage, 1980); Ann Rosen Spector is a psychologist with Women in Transition in Philadelphia; and Dr. Patricia Wisch is a psychologist in private practice in Philadelphia.

HOW TO RAISE
YOUR MAN

INTRODUCTION

We thought that when we became new style women we would share everything fifty-fifty with our men. We-e-e-ll, maybe sixty-forty. So how come there are still so many households in which seventy-thirty would be an improvement? (Did you say eighty-twenty?)

This is the problem: even though women have made great strides toward equal treatment at work and at school, and even though there have been huge leaps in the law, a great many women complain that they are only running in place at home. Whether the guy is younger generation or older generation doesn't seem to matter. The situation, alas, is much the same. She is still, as always, concerned about his interests, but finds he isn't as interested in her concerns. She caters, as usual, to his needs, but when she needs him, he isn't always there.

And women are not as willing as they once were to shrug this off by saying, "That's how men are." Now they are asking, "Is that how men have to be?" Now they are saying, "This is ridiculous!"

The gloom-and-doomers are much in evidence. Susan Burstein, an advertising agency vice-president, wrote to the *Chicago Sun-Times* to complain that the "right" that women have won in their battle to be equal is the right to do "double work, with double responsibility, and no help in sight."

HOW TO RAISE YOUR MAN

Frances Lear, president of a consulting firm (and wife of TV producer Norman Lear) wrote to the *New York Times* to state that a woman has only the choice between "submissiveness" and "going it alone." She wrote, "A woman who dares ask for more equitable treatment from the man she loves will lose that man to another woman who won't seek to change the rules."

Women wonder and worry whether such statements are true. Says mental health administrator Naomi Dank, "Now that women are aware that there is a brass ring to grab, they fear that grabbing it will mean losing their marriage... or the possibility of marriage." But she warns that "giving in to that fear is self-defeating."

No question about it. Women cannot simply ignore the change that has taken place in themselves. They can't pretend it hasn't happened. You can't stuff toothpaste back in the tube. You have to figure out what to do with it now.

Admittedly, some men really are hopeless. But it is wrong, even outrageous, to suggest that all, or even most, are. Many men are ready to grow and change, to become happier themselves by making the woman they love happier. They just need to be shown how.

How many men am I talking about? Well, more than women believe and more than men will admit in public, I'd say.

And so I would like to provide some suggestions on how a woman can encourage this growth and this kind of change in the man she loves and also grow and change herself. The suggestions in this book come from psychologists, psychiatrists, and marriage counselors as well as from ordinary couples and from my experience in my own mar-

INTRODUCTION

riage. I have discovered that there are things I do that I do right, and I'm not shy about passing the good news along.

The fact that I am lighthearted about a subject that makes so many women heavyhearted does not mean I don't take the matter seriously. It simply indicates that I have read some of the weightier manuals on male-female relationships and I can understand why people might prefer to stay miserable rather than plow through them.

I look at it this way: experience has shown that it feels better to laugh than to cry. And that you get better results if you try rather than give up. If anything that follows encourages a reader to laugh and try rather than give up and cry—that is no bad thing.

Rose DeWolf

1

THESE ARE THE TIMES THAT TRY WOMEN'S SOULS

I have realized for some time that in a very critical area of human relationships—man and woman together—I am out of step with my times. The problem is that I don't complain about my husband.

And let me tell you, I have very mixed emotions about that. I suddenly understand the feelings of a college pal of mine who had been drafted. On one hand, he didn't want to go into the army because he wanted to go to graduate school. On the other hand, he was relieved—even pleased—to know that someday, when all the guys were sitting around swapping old army stories, at least he'd have something to say.

Moaning about one's mate is the trendiest trend going, and I'm left out. I complained to my husband about this. I told him he wasn't giving me anything to talk to my friends about. "If you really feel bad about it," he said helpfully, "say anything you want, and I'll swear it's true." I'm going to *complain* about someone like that? Clearly, my situation is hopeless.

However, as a journalist, I have always made a point of keeping on top of current trends even when I'm not personally participating in one. You know, one year it's premature ejaculation; the next year it's celibacy. One year you can't pick up a magazine without finding an article on depression; the next year the officially sanctioned form of suffering is stress. And if you get depressed in the wrong year, you feel not only blue but dated as well.

Right now I notice that women are suffering from a feeling of being...well...mistreated by their men. Over and over I hear the complaint that "my husband [boyfriend, lover, roommate—pick one] doesn't understand me. What *I* want, what *I* need doesn't seem to count with him—not enough, anyway."

It pops out in the kind of articles that appear in women's magazines: "What to Do If Your Husband Doesn't Make Love to You Often Enough." And in the kind of dialogue you hear on TV: "You never listen to anything I say." Even newly wed Mindy complained to Mork: "I don't know how to make you hear what I'm saying" (indicating that even after the Martians invade, earthling women will still have the same problems).

I hear it when I eavesdrop on buses: "I can't seem to get through to Harvey how important this is to me." And, of course, I hear it from my friends.

Take Melanie, who is a very glamorous TV personality. She came home after a terrible day at the studio—one of those days when the celebrity she was supposed to interview showed up late, when a camera boom (or something) fell on her foot. She was weary, she was wretched, she was worn. Surely, all of this showed in her expressive eyes, in her slumped shoulders, in the fact that she limped.

Well, it happened that on this day she and her husband arrived at their apartment building at exactly the same time. They met at the elevator. She waited for him to say something, which he did. Looking up from his newspaper, he asked, "What's for dinner?"

THE TIMES THAT TRY WOMEN'S SOULS

Now, it isn't that this husband and wife don't have a good marriage. They do. It isn't that she doesn't love him. She does. Even so, she did think at that moment of nudging him down the elevator shaft. She had this wonderful fantasy of seeing him bounce off the bottom. He would stumble to his knees, bruised, scratched, aching, and wondering what the hell had happened. And she would lean her head into the shaft and call down to him: "Pot ro-o-o-oast!"

I checked out my own observations with experts (as journalists are wont to do), and they confirmed a growing unhappiness among the women of the land. The Couples Learning Center in suburban Philadelphia did a four-year study of 235 "average" couples and discovered, among other things, that 80 percent of the men were perfectly satisfied with their marriage but only 29 percent of the women said the same thing.

New York psychiatrist Anne Locksley interviewed 2,300 married persons to determine how they saw their relationships and found that, overwhelmingly, the wives had negative feelings. They felt left out. They felt misunderstood. The wives, far more often than the husbands, complained about a sense of "distance" between them.

Clearly, after at least a decade of pronouncements about how couples are now more open with each other, about how the roles of the sexes have changed, despite the fact that women become police officers and men are learning to cook, despite the fact that both sexes can now wear the same kind of jeans, the age-old relationship between men and women is still quite the same in many fundamental respects. Which is to say that the men fundamentally expect the women to respect *their* wishes and not vice versa.

Okay, so this isn't as dramatic a problem as being married to a dope addict or a bank robber or a fellow who keeps a mistress or a brute who beats you or a mystic who takes a vow of chastity on his wedding night. But I'm not one who thinks you can't cry about a bad haircut just because some other people are bald.

I say if the man you love doesn't understand where you are coming from—unless it's the kitchen—you ought to do more than complain. You ought to do something about it.

But more on that later.

You might claim that the problem I'm talking about here is nothing new. You might say that men have never understood women, and that's true. But in the past, women didn't *expect* to be understood. That's a big difference.

You don't mope about a problem if you don't know you have one. Maybe before television was invented, some people thought it would be nice to have pictures on their radio; maybe in the days when covered wagons crossed the plains, some people wished there were wings on the wagon to cut the trip to six hours instead of six months. If you didn't have these things, however, you didn't necessarily feel deprived!

Love can be looked at in the same context.

It can be argued that, for most people, love is a recent invention. Throughout history, what most men and women worried about was sheer survival—their own and that of the human race. When you have to worry where your next meal is coming from, you tend not to spend a lot of time wondering whether that certain someone will have a special look in his eye.

THE TIMES THAT TRY WOMEN'S SOULS

Scholars of such matters point out that romance is a function of leisure and a decent living. It is, apparently, no great coincidence that the romantic stories handed down through generations almost always involve princes and princesses, lords and ladies—that is to say, those with leisure and a decent living. Yorick the Peasant, out working the fields twenty hours a day, wasn't much concerned about a meaningful relationship.

Think about it. Even dear little Cinderella, stuck cleaning out the fireplace, came from a rich family. If that had not been the case, it isn't likely the prince would have sent an invitation to the ball to her address in the first place. Even in fairy tales, the common folk dance only in the streets—not in the palace. Just because her stepmother made a maid out of Cindy didn't mean the family couldn't afford servants. Cindy could afford to think about going to balls.

You have to have a certain standard of living to be able to mess around with fairy godmothers and elves and magic potions and all that. You have to have time in which to dream of finding your heart's desire. I think a case can be made for the theory that the modern preoccupation with falling in love is a by-product of the forty-hour week. However...

There still are those who give a higher priority to practical considerations than to emotional ones. A woman I know, who is fifty, told her mother, who is eighty, that her husband had left her. The old lady said, "Ethel, you're better off. He was a no-goodnik, that one. He never made a decent living. He never supported you and the kids right. He's a bum. Good riddance to him." And Ethel said, "But

Ma, I love him." To which her mother replied, "Love? Love? What's that got to do with anything?"

No way to explain.

But if expecting to have, wanting to have love is a relatively recent invention, the desire to be "understood"—to be considered, as the saying goes, "a person in my own right"—is even newer.

For years, the prevailing wisdom on the capability of men to understand women, passed on from mother to daughter, could have been summed up this way: "That's how they are, the unfeeling clods." In other words, you didn't expect much, and thus you couldn't be that disappointed when you didn't get it. A woman was supposed to find happiness, not in being understood by her man, but in learning to understand him.

The fact that women now seem to expect greater sensitivity from their men and more of a partnership feeling in their relationships indicates that social history is in the making. Women have obviously changed—not as much as some would like, but not as little as others claim. It's still the wife who spends the most time with the children (while the husband comments that she is too easy with them or that she yells too much). If couples gather at a private home for dinner, it is almost always the women (even the most "liberated" ones) who jump after the last course to offer to clear dishes and help clean up.

Yet somehow or other, women increasingly are saying that they want back some of the stroking and encouragement they've been giving out. They don't want to feel that, if they decide to do something for themselves, they should feel guilty or apologize.

THE TIMES THAT TRY WOMEN'S SOULS

There is no shortage of theories on why this is so, but it hardly makes much difference which explanation wins out. What matters is what's going on, and complaining is what's going on. The message I get is that new style women don't want to give up their old style men. They don't want to trade them in on new models; they just want to get a few dents out and maybe a new paint job.

What women would prefer, I don't doubt, is some kind of instant treatment akin to the kind of "beauty makeover" common to women's magazines. You know, first you see the "before"—limp hair, grim expression, clothes two sizes too large, and what's more, the photograph is out of focus. Then Mr. Kenneth or M. Antoine or some such takes her in hand. Her eyebrows are plucked, her hair is styled, her makeup is changed, her clothes fit, she's lost fifty pounds, the "after" photo's in focus, and she's smiling.

Of course.

In the case of the men, what is desired is more of a "psyche make-over." You might start out, say, with a man who is a little tight in the wallet, a little loose after a few drinks, long on working but short on talking things out with his mate. The experts take a little nip here, a tiny tuck there, and possibly change his shaving lotion, and *voila!* Now he's new style. He has been transformed by the experts into a sympathetic, concerned, understanding, and supportive man. (Also cheerful, thrifty, clean, brave, and reverent. He was a Boy Scout in his youth.)

Terrific.

"Would you send Bernie in?" a friend asked when I mused on this aloud. (Bernie is my husband.) "It wouldn't be worth the postage," I said. "He's already sympathetic, concerned, understanding, and supportive. Most of the time. And I like his brand of shaving lotion."

That got us into a discussion of what one does to develop this kind of guy, this kind of relationship. "What do you do?" she asked me.

I replied, "Nothing." At the time my only theory on how to have a reasonable relationship was "Find the right guy." I felt that was the whole story of Bernie and me. I found this man by sheer dumb luck, and he had turned out to be a very state-of-the-art sort. I hadn't tried to figure out how or why it happened. I was too busy rubbing my rabbit's foot and stashing four-leaf clovers in my dresser.

It wasn't that I had everything my way or that we never had differences or that we continuously floated through life on clouds... merely that we seemed to share a lot. Merely that I felt he would support me in something I wanted even if it wasn't something he thought important. What more was there to say? Plenty more, as it turns out.

As time went on and as I kept getting that left-out feeling every time the conversation turned to women feeling left out, I began to wonder if maybe there *is* something I do—and that others who seem to live in similar mutuality do—that encourages this result.

So I interviewed counselors and other couples and talked it over with Bernie, too. I read books and journals. And I discovered there are some things I do—even if unwittingly, even if not all the time, even if not as well as I might—that I do right. I amazed myself.

This is not to say I was wrong about the importance of finding the "right guy." I still believe that, and I admit that I don't believe you can easily rescue a "wrong" one. I mean, I put statements like "The love of a good woman will straighten him out," or "Once he has family responsibilities he'll be a changed man," or "He isn't *really* like that, not deep down, you'll see," in the same category with "The check is in the mail," and "I left it in my other suit," and "Peace in our time." Possible, but most unlikely.

What I learned, however, is that even though you cannot change a frog into a prince with a kiss (sigh), with a little effort you can get your prince to treat you more royally. In other words, you can't change a personality, but you can influence behavior. And this, it seems to me, is what I do when I do what I didn't know I did. I checked this out with Prince Bernard, who agrees. It seems I have always taken for granted two things that many other women ignore:

1. That it's okay for me to want something.
2. That the man in my life may be perfectly willing for me to have that something, or may be able to be convinced that I should have it, and indeed may help me get it... at least part of the time.

I have found that an incredible number of women remain frustrated and dissatisfied because they don't take this simple (well, I think it's simple) attitude.

Like my friend Phyllis.

Phyllis's outlook has changed in recent years, but she admits that for a long time she was her own worst enemy. She had been a full-time wife and mother for some time when she got this idea that she'd like to go to law school. She "just knew" her husband Tim wouldn't go for it. She just knew her relatives would be horrified at the idea that she would even think of leaving hearth and home before the youngest child was thirty-two. (He was then four.)

So she said nothing. But she thought about it. More accurately, she stewed about it, chafing at the unfairness of it all, internally plotting how she would exact her revenge.

Then one night she and Tim were at a party at which one of the women said she was thinking of going to medical school. Tim said, "That's a wonderful idea. You should do it."

Two weeks later Phyllis got up the nerve to mention her own ambition to Tim. It took two weeks because she reasoned that just because Tim thought somebody else's wife should go to medical school didn't prove he thought his own wife should study law. But, as it happened, that was just what he thought.

Phyllis enrolled. The relatives were just as shocked as she thought they would be, but Tim didn't have a qualm. And Phyllis was so grateful, it was pitiful. She made a vow that her husband and children would never notice a change in their lives because she was going to school. She would stay up later and get up earlier to get all her chores done. If Tim came home with friends after golf, there was Phyllis setting out refreshments as any good wife would do. There was Phyllis watching the children to make sure they did not (as the relatives predicted) turn into dope fiends, libertines, dropouts, or members of some wild cult. Although Phyllis almost did. She was that tired.

"I can't believe the guilt trip I put on myself," she says now.

Phyllis may have gotten what she wanted but she sure did suffer in the getting of it. And all because, she admits now as she looks back, she felt so guilty about *wanting* it. She didn't think she deserved what she wanted—not to the point of asking anyone else to make sacrifices for her, that is, even though she made sacrifices for them.

She didn't even have to face Tim pounding on a table yelling, *"Never!"* Her children did not put in a request for transfer to an orphanage. Were they to be expected to *turn down* the super treatment they got from her? If she had sandwiches prepared, were they supposed to refuse to eat them as a matter of principle? Would you?

Might they not have pitched in and helped if Phyllis had asked them to? Would they have done without so that she could "do"? Phyllis now thinks so. And wishes she had at least tried to find out back then. She never gave her family a chance. And what's more she might never have given herself a chance if she hadn't been emboldened by that fleeting conversation at the party. Incidentally, the other woman never did go to medical school.

It is well known, of course, that no one can put limits on you as tightly as you can put them on yourself. This is not something limited to the female sex. Men do it all the time. A guy will want to ask Adorable Alice for a date, but he's so sure she will turn him down—and humiliatingly, too ("Drop dead, creep")—that he never asks her. She never finds out he is interested. He will never find out whether she *might* have been interested in him. Many men talk themselves out of opportunities ("I couldn't handle it; there's no point in trying."), but just because this is an equal opportunity disaster does not excuse women from practicing it with the one person who they should assume has their best interests at heart.

I may not always get what I want, but it wouldn't occur to me not to try for it. What do you gain from deciding to stay miserable? You can't even win an award from the Masochists' League, because there isn't one.

It seems to me that a woman should always give a guy credit for wanting her to be happy. Why? Because he usually does. We aren't talking about some vicious beast, some cruel Neanderthal who enjoys making women suffer. Well, let's hope not anyway. We are talking about a fellow who wants to be with you as much as you want to be with him.

After all, it was the majority of *men* who said they were happy with their marriages. What's more, a recent study of widows and widowers by Johns Hopkins University scientists showed that the loss of a mate doesn't affect the death rate of women at all, but men are noticeably unable to make it alone. Maybe wives should come stamped with the label *Caution: Loss of this person can be hazardous to your health.*

A man may not want to change his habits, customs, comforts, whatever. If everything is going his way, why would he want to change? But that is not to say he *won't* make some compromises, try some new ways of doing things, agree to be accommodating, and reach out to you if he has good reason. The happiness of a loved one is a very good reason.

Psychiatrist Aaron Beck says husbands sometimes tell him, "I don't see any problem, so why should I do any of these fool things my wife wants? I don't see any reason to change." And Beck will reply, "You don't have to do anything you don't want to. Of course, you'll come home every night to a wife who is unhappy and hostile. Your kids will probably grow up neurotic. You could end up paying psychiatrists for them and a divorce lawyer for yourself. But look, it's a free country. If you don't want to do something, don't do it."

Sooner or later, men usually realize that what is important to the woman in their life is important to them, too. Marriage counselors say that it is invariably the woman who brings a couple into therapy. He comes in saying, "I don't know why she's griping. But if she wants to try this, I'll humor her." Then he becomes even more enthusiastic about examining their relationship than she is.

Interestingly, a study of a cross-section of American couples, commissioned by Connecticut Mutual Life Insurance Company, has found that both husbands and wives today claim they want a more equal marriage. Obviously, the husbands who said this are hiding it well.

In fact, everything I have heard, read, or experienced tells me that if a woman wants her man to understand her, if she wants to get as well as give, she must first give herself permission to want change and then she must create the kind of atmosphere that encourages and enables him to change. As a starter, she must immediately banish from her thoughts such self-defeating phrases as:

> *He'll never.*
> *He can't.*
> *He won't.*
>
> Or:
> *Him? You've got to be kidding.*

Give yourself a chance by giving him a chance.

2

GIVING A MIRACLE A CHANCE TO HAPPEN

Once upon a time there was a couple whose major complaint was that they didn't see enough of each other. She worked nine to five in an office. He worked weird hours as a police detective. She always had weekends off. He usually got Sunday and Monday. This meant that having two consecutive days together was a luxury they only dreamed about.

But then one week, lo! the incredible happened. He would be off on Saturday, too. And so, although normally she would devote Saturdays to doing laundry, cleaning, shopping, and such, this time she made sure to have every chore out of the way by 10:00 A.M.—at which hour she found her beloved cheerfully packing his gym bag, preparatory to going off to spend the day with the guys.

Uh-oh.

Our heroine felt like running into her room and having a good cry. She felt like screaming at him, "You no good parcel of bird droppings! You are the one who always complains about our being apart so much. But when we finally get two days together, *what do you do?*"

As it happened, she did not do either. Instead, she cooled her outrage just long enough to say, "You know what I wish? I wish you'd stay home so we could do something together."

And he said, "Oh? Okay."

As easy as that. It turned out he'd assumed that because she *always* did the laundry, shopping, and cleaning on Saturday, she'd want him out of her way. He was just as glad to know otherwise.

Now, I would be the first to admit that just because this particular story ended well does not mean such an ending is guaranteed. Cynics have been very quick to point out to me that there were lots of other things our hero could have said.

Like: "Gosh, I wish I'd known you were going to be available. But it's too late now. I've already promised the guys I'd come."

Or: "I'm sorry, but I'd really rather to go to the gym today. We'll do something together tomorrow."

Or (the brute!): "Don't hassle me. I'm going."

Or even (the fiend!): "The truth is, I'm not going to the gym at all. Actually, I am running away to Tahiti with Torchy, the topless dancer from the Boom-Boom Room."

You might argue that this little episode would never have occurred in the first place if he had asked her in advance if she would be available on Saturday. Or if she had told him in advance that she was going to be free. All very true.

You could also take the position that, to have a truly happy ending to this story, he should have offered to *share* those miserable rotten chores he assumed would keep her so busy.

I am the first to agree that the possibilities are endless. I can even think of more. Just at the critical moment, the

GIVING A MIRACLE A CHANCE TO HAPPEN

telephone could ring. It's his long lost twin brother. Or suddenly, they would hear a mysterious scream. Or World War III could break out.

But so what? What *did* happen is that by merely letting our hero know what she wanted instead of assuming that he knew and either didn't care or wouldn't do it anyway, our heroine got what she wanted. Which was, of course, our hero.

It's so simple, you have to wonder why people don't always do it. Why don't I always do it, now that I think of it?

Assuming that you can't get what you want—and therefore not even bothering to ask—is a very common human failing. Bernie always accuses me of turning down jobs I haven't even been offered yet, or haven't applied for, for that matter. Hasn't everybody at some time heard "Why didn't you *say* something?" or "How was I to know?" or the ever popular "What am I, a mind reader?" or even "But I thought that you thought that I thought that you..."

The proprietor of a fabric shop in my neighborhood has told me that, because he keeps most of his goods in a back room, he has a sign on the front counter that says, "If you don't see what you want, ask for it." But even though that sign is there, even though he also tells customers directly that what they see is *not* all they can get, some people never get the message. If what they want isn't right under their nose, he says, they decide it isn't there and they leave. Only later do they say, "You mean you had that all the time? Oh, gosh, I wish I'd known."

I am not trying to tell you that only women do this.

I know that's not true. I once worked for a newspaper that suddenly had a job opening in its Washington bureau because somebody had retired after working there for fifty years. This was considered a really plum assignment, and for a week the office buzzed with speculation over just who the editor would select. We figured it had to be one of three stars on the staff—Joe, the best investigative reporter, or Neil who covered the state capital, or Mark who was our man in City Hall. Joe and Neil and Mark figured that, too. But when the notice went up on the bulletin board, the job went to Jerry, a comparative unknown who had been slogging away on the night shift. Nobody had even thought of Jerry, except the editor, of course. In time, I asked that editor why he had picked Jerry, and he said, "He was the only one who asked for the job. I thought no one else was interested."

Oh.

It is bad enough to do this with storekeepers and strangers and employers with whom we are not on intimate terms. You wouldn't think this also happens at home. But, of course, it does, and much more often, I suspect, with women than with men.

Men do seem to spell out their wants pretty well when they are inside their castle. Sort of like the Cookie Monster on Sesame Street: "Bring me cookie. I want cookie." A man is likely to say, "I've had a rough day, and what I need is a beer"—and expect his wife, lover, or butler to hand it to him. A woman, however, might say, "I've had a rough day," and then wait.

Does she want him to commiserate? To take her to

dinner? To offer to take the kids to the zoo? To donate the kids to the zoo? To offer *her* a beer?

How is he supposed to know what she wants if she doesn't tell him?

I've had conversations where a friend will say, "Oh, c'mon. He *knows*. He just doesn't care. He only cares when it concerns him."

That's possible, of course. But is she really sure? I wish I had a dime for every time I've been wrong when I thought I was sure what Bernie would say or do. I am very often right. I know him very well. Even so...

I have found that I get better results—not perfect, but better—with a find-out-first, get-mad-later (if necessary) policy. I get better results by speaking up as opposed to waiting around for my thought waves to get through. Let us say, to take a very simple example, that what I want is a hug. A hug is generally what I do want after a tough day. I am totally convinced of the therapeutic value of hugs. I think they are generally underappreciated in the scheme of things, and it's a darned shame, too.

Really, now. There are six million books on the subject of sexual intercourse. How to do it. When to do it. Where to do it and with whom. Every conceivable question on conception is explored. There are probably ten thousand books on the missionary position alone, including statements on the official position of the missionary profession.

There are also detailed analyses of kissing. Hollywood historians are very big on this. Who kisses best, worst, least, longest. Anthropologists study kissing in various cultures. Does rubbing noses equal touching lips? Stuff like that.

There are even articles on coming to grips with groping. But hugs tend to be shrugged off. When I asked a couple of men at work who they considered the greatest hugger in history, one said Yogi Bear; the other thought I said "mugger" and nominated Jack the Ripper. Boo.

There is a bumper sticker that says: "Have you hugged a green plant today?" A green plant? If you hug a plant, you could break the stem. If you don't hug somebody you love, you can break his or her heart. Where are our priorities? Hugging is easy to do and can be done almost anywhere, which is more than can be said for certain other forms of affection. Hugging is a terrific tension reliever, better than Valium and certainly more fun.

But all of this is getting away from what I started out to say, which is that whenever I want a hug, I say so. I never wait for Bernie to notice that I am looking wistful. I don't hang about waiting for him to guess what I am thinking. I don't take any chances that he will guess wrong. No subtle hints either. I say: "Help! I need a hug. *Now.* Emergency! Fading fast. Quick!" And all things being equal, Bernie will find the time and a way to oblige.

Whatever I want, large or small, whenever I need Bernie's cooperation, even when I think it's something he probably won't be thrilled about, even if I know it will be a hassle for him, even if I'm positive he will think I've gone berserk, I let him know. And what happens after that depends on—well, what happens after that.

If you are the type who takes this sort of thing for granted, you may well wonder why others do not.

Lots of reasons. There is, for example, the unarguable

fact that, quite often, when a woman says that a guy will be upset by what she asks, he *will* be upset; that when she predicts he will give her a hard time, she knows whereof she speaks; that when she says the lout cares only about himself, then he *is* a lout who cares only about himself. They say, "I'm just being realistic."

Some women won't say what they want just because they think it's unromantic. I know that some women would scoff: "You *ask* for a hug? Phooey." What they want is someone who knows without being told that they would like a bouquet. They want someone who will sense their restlessness or dissatisfaction and sweep them into their arms or off to Paris as any half respectable hero of a romantic novel would do.

And some women won't spell out what they want because they're afraid of being embarrassed. Nobody enjoys a kick in the self-esteem. What if he not only objects but also laughs? What if he thinks it's stupid? What if it *is* stupid?

There are women who are afraid to say what they want because it is so fundamental ("I want to share in decisions" or "I want you to stay home more") that they are afraid he will react by leaving them. They believe their only choice is to go along or go it alone. More than one woman has said to me, "The men have the upper hand, and they know it. They know that if they leave, they'll be pursued." Sociologist John Scanzoni says this fear increases along with the man's income if the wife knows she won't be able to maintain the same standard of living on her own. And heaven knows, the situation is hardly improved by the host of males who write articles warning wives that the reason men like mistresses so much is that they "don't make demands."

Mistress don't make demands? Who are they kidding? What about diamonds? What about mink coats? What about marriage?

But even if it's true that women have lots of reasons for not just up and saying what they'd like, it's also true that most of the reasons aren't as good as they like to think. For instance, the woman who "knows" he'll be upset may be wrong. I know we pride ourselves on being supersensitive. There are, after all, all those studies that show that women are much more sensitive, much more intuitive than men. But "more than" is not always. How many times can a woman actually guess what a man is thinking? Says psychiatrist and marriage counselor David Reed, "If a woman says she can do it two times out of ten, possible. If she says five times out of ten, she and her husband must be very close. If she says ten out of ten, she's lying in her teeth."

Admit it. Have you *never* been surprised? It usually happens to me just when I am absolutely positive about how Bernie will react. One time I got a phone call from a friend who was in the middle of a divorce, and she told me that she had decided to move back to Philadelphia and resume her career here. Well, she and I are very close, and I wanted to invite her to stay with us until she found an apartment. But I didn't. Because just at that time, Bernie was working nights as well as days on a project with a very close deadline. He had papers all over the place, and he was under a lot of pressure. I knew that, much as he likes Karen, a houseguest just then was out of the question.

GIVING A MIRACLE A CHANCE TO HAPPEN

But what do I know, really? When I merely mentioned to Bernie that Karen planned to move back to Philadelphia, he said, "What she should do is stay with us until she can get settled." And she did.

My friend Angel tells a story about the night a parking lot attendant lost the key to her car. He hoped she carried a spare, but no such luck. "There was no way around it," she said. "I had to call Jimmy and ask him to come and get me. And I knew he'd have a fit. He had to drive an hour to get there, and he wouldn't be home in time to watch a game he wanted to see on TV. I knew he wasn't going to be happy. In fact, knowing Jim, I was sure he'd take that parking lot attendant apart. I even apologized in advance for the scene Jim was going to make. I had that attendant so scared he was shaking. Then in comes Jim. He's all smiles. He says, 'Don't worry about it. It can happen to anybody.'"

My friend Julie adds a tale about the day she spent brooding about something John had done. She can't even remember what it was now. But that day she was so angry that she decided to have it out with him the second he came home. And just to make sure she didn't forget anything, she wrote out an entire speech. "I knew what he was going to say. I knew every excuse he would make, so I had all my answers prepared. But no sooner had I started when he said, 'I did that? I didn't realize. I'm sorry. I don't blame you for being angry. I'll never do it again.' I still had three whole pages to go," recalls Julie. "And all the best parts, too. What frustration!"

And about this business of not wanting to speak up

because it's not romantic. Marriage counselor Sally Green has a sign over her desk that reads, "If you really loved me, you would read my mind." Sure, it's a lovely notion—a couple so close that each knows instinctively what the other would like. Two minds so in tune that he hands her a cup of coffee before she reaches for it. Two people so in love that he knows exactly how to respond to her every mood. "Don't speak, my darling," he says. "I know." And he does know. Everything. "It should be that way," says Sally Green, "but it's not." How true.

So why torture yourself about it? Even if it would be more romantic to be surprised with flowers, is it really so unromantic to ask for them and then get them? "Your request is my command," says the gallant knight. And even if the knight forgets the flowers, it could be because he had a hard day slaying dragons. If that happened to me, I'd ask again.

Even if I felt embarrassed about asking. Even if what I want sounds stupid and is stupid. I figure that if the man I love won't make allowances for me, who will? And don't I make allowances for him? I try to keep firmly in mind, too, that although I have many times threatened to die of embarrassment, I'm not dead yet.

Which brings us to the most fearful inhibitor of all—that deep-down inner belief that if we make a request he finds offensive, he will pack his bags and leave. Just because you asked? Sure, with very serious differences of opinion, there is the possibility of serious alienation. But just for *saying something*? I don't believe it. Not unless he was halfway out the door anyway.

GIVING A MIRACLE A CHANCE TO HAPPEN

Women have been sold the idea that men do not value a solid relationship. They are alleged to be playboys always on the lookout for someone younger and more beautiful, precariously susceptible to a wink or a wave. But when I look around, that isn't what I see. I see guys who, even if they don't want to admit it, need us as much as we need them.

I think the problem is that the playboy type has won much too much publicity. The less exciting, but more comforting, truth is that a man will love a woman even if she is not beautiful or even a good cook. The mass of men love women through illness and burned roasts, through arguments and excess poundage, despite in-laws, outlaws, and tax laws. And not enough attention is paid to that.

There is a theory, you know, that when you expect the best, as opposed to the worst, it is more likely to happen. As George Bernard Shaw said, "The difference between a flower girl and a lady is how she is treated." In his play *Pygmalion*, which was the basis for the musical *My Fair Lady*, a flower girl dressed, talked, and behaved like a lady and was treated like a princess. She created the positive vibes, you might say, that guided others in reacting to her.

If Eliza Doolittle had said, "There's no point in my trying to improve my lot in life, because nothing can happen," that would have been the end of the play.

Actually, I think (and psychologists I talked to back me up in this) there can be even *more* danger in *not* letting the man you love know what you want. Because, well, that isn't playing fair. What generally happens is that just because you haven't given someone a chance to straighten something out does not mean you won't hold a grudge against him for not doing so.

There is an old movie, *The Snows of Kilimanjaro,* starring Gregory Peck and Ava Gardner (based, of course, on the short story by Ernest Hemingway), where the plot revolves around a wife's inability to straight-out tell her husband what she wants.

In this movie, Gregory is a writer who loves Africa. He likes to hear lions roar and rhinoceroses call to each other. And he is just thrilled when he gets an opportunity to go on a safari. He tells his wife (Ava) about it, and we can tell she is not thrilled at all. Ava doesn't want to go on a safari. She wants to stay home and have a baby. In fact, she has just learned she is pregnant.

"Darling," she says tentatively. But Gregory is oblivious to all but his own excitement. "Shhh," he says, "don't talk it all away." So Ava does not tell him she is pregnant. She hints a little: "Wouldn't it be nice to have children?" He replies, "Yes, but later."

Well, Ava being a loyal old style wife—this movie was made thirty or so years ago—dutifully throws herself down the stairs to induce a miscarriage. Only in the movies, of course, is this technique effective. At the hospital where Ava is taken, a doctor tells Gregory that the baby is lost. "What baby?" Gregory gasps. The doctor is disgusted. "Don't you people talk to each other?" he says. You tell 'em, Doc.

That's not the end. Ava feels guilty. She starts to drink. Gregory feels guilty. He starts to drink. Ava wants revenge. She starts to snipe at him. He wants revenge. He starts to play around. They are both miserable. Finally, she leaves him. And it takes an entire movie to get them back together for one ardent clinch before she dies. Sigh. See what can happen if you don't speak up? A word to the wise.

It is entirely possible that a man will be relieved to find out what the woman in his life wants. It is possible he will say, "Is that all?"

I think this issue of speaking up is particularly relevant for women today. Because even though we know that women have changed, everybody knows that men have not. And so, although we may be assertive in other arenas, we are not necessarily assertive in that last battlefront of the war for women's equality—the home front. Why bother, we say to ourselves. We all know what men are like, don't we?

Maybe yes. Maybe no. Those two words "everybody knows" have gotten more people into trouble than rubber checks.

I'm not saying that what "everybody knows" is never true. In fact, I've been told by police investigators that what-everybody-knows is one of law enforcement's best friends. If the word is going around that there is something fishy going on in Harry's Flounder Shop, there probably is. I once talked to a former U.S. attorney for New Jersey who had just sent a couple dozen crooked politicians away for a period of meditation. I asked him how he had known just which pols to investigate. And he said he began by looking closely at those about whom it was widely said, "He's the best that money can buy." What everybody knows often turns out to be true.

But not always, of course. Which is why gossip alone is not sufficient for sending somebody to jail. There is this requirement for evidence and proof and such. There is a need to check the story out. What is true in general may not be true in an individual case.

That is all I am suggesting here: that you can't take what-everybody-knows to be true without checking. For example, everybody knows that you can't tell a man that sex with him is not absolutely perfect in every way. Everybody knows that the male ego is too fragile to survive such information. Everybody knows that the least suggestion that you would like, say, a little more warming up in the bull pen before he throws his final pitch, would end his ballplaying career forever.

But as we have all found out after we discover that the new china is marked "too fragile to go in the dishwasher" only *after* it has been through the dishwasher and survived, there is fragile and there is *Fragile*. You don't have to be insulting. You can say, "Mmmmmmmmmm, you know what I'd like?"

I admit that I am particularly sensitive to this issue of what-everyone-knows, because in my life it generally turns out that everyone knows but me. This is not the case when I am working as a reporter. When I'm on duty, I'm sensitive to every nuance, I listen closely, I question, I take notes, I notice the expressions on people's faces. If I may be so immodest as to say so, I've been told I do this very well. But for some strange reason this does not carry over into, as they say, Real Life.

In Real Life I am always someplace else when what-everybody-knows is going on. At the office, I will say, "Where's Billy?" And a colleague will say, "Billy? Heck, he

GIVING A MIRACLE A CHANCE TO HAPPEN

quit eight months ago after that big fight he had with the editor. It was the talk of the office for weeks." What big fight? I am positive I was not locked up in the ladies' room for weeks, and yet, somehow I missed it all. Rats.

When Bernie and I go to a party, it is Bernie who notices everything. On the way home, he says, "Whew, how about that Dennie? It's not like him to drink so much. He was so crocked he could barely stand up. Isn't a shame about Melvin and Maude. It's obvious that marriage is on the rocks. Harry doesn't look well at all. I hope he's all right."

What? Why wasn't I invited to the same party he went to? I mean, I talked to Dennie. I met Melvin and Maude. I spent twenty minutes with Harry. I didn't notice a thing. But sure enough, the next time I see Dennie, he talks about the load he had on at the party. The next thing I hear, Melvin and Maude have split, and Harry has had his gall bladder out. I can't stand it.

I tell myself that Bernie is as observant as he is because he is in the business of being observant. If he is negotiating a labor contract, it is important that he notice every nuance in what the other side says, to notice in a fleeting expression that a concession might be at hand. Good cardplayers have the same ability. They can tell from a nervous tic on the left side of the right eye that the other player is bluffing. But I, too, am in the business of being observant, and it doesn't seem to help me. If a policeman asked me whether I got the license number of a speeding car, I would probably reply, "Car? What car?"

Because I so often do not know what-everybody-knows,

I am sympathetic to men who don't know what the women in their lives *think* they know. This is why I am not at all sympathetic when a friend says to me in expressions so common they have become clichés, "If he had cared, he would have noticed. It was as plain as the nose on his face." Or "It had to hit you the minute you walked in the room. It was so obvious, it was incredible." And the old reliable, "What am I supposed to do, hit him over the head with it?"

I am glad you asked that question. The answer is yes. Well, don't hit him on the head, exactly. Just say something. Don't assume he knows what you know or that he is like what everybody knows men are like.

When I hear women say, "My Joe would never go for that; I wouldn't even bring it up," or "There's no point in mentioning it because it wouldn't do any good," I just despair. Because even though I know they are probably right, I also know there is always this itsy-bitsy, teeny-weeny chance they are not. And if they don't *say something* they will never find out.

Therefore, here is my plan. Before you sulk, scream, sock him in the nose, or serve notice that your lawyer will call in the morning, say to him, "You know what I'd like?" He might just say, "Oh? Okay."

Even if it's true that more times than not it won't work. Even though it's true that it is only a first step. Sometimes the first step is all you need. It's been my experience that even if you truly believe that it would "take a miracle" for this man to do what you would like, you owe it to yourself to give that miracle a chance to happen.

GIVING A MIRACLE A CHANCE TO HAPPEN

Before you can win a contest, you have to enter it. Before your own special genie can grant your three wishes, you have to tell him what they are. And, what the heck, rub him three times, too.

3

NEW STYLE, OLD STYLE

My friends and I do not agree on exactly what constitutes a new style man. We agree in principle, but not on the specifics. Not at all.

A lot has already been written, of course, about the difference between traditional and modern men and women, but unfortunately a lot of that has been hostile, unhelpful, and wrong.

For one thing, there is a notion that we have to be clearly modern or unmistakably traditional, when in fact, on a scale of one to ten, most of us fall somewhere in between.

Some people seem to think that new style can be determined by whether or not a woman works or whether a man does needlepoint and is willing to cry. But those are choices anyone can make. The real thing goes much deeper than that.

There are those who would dismiss the matter by saying that a new style woman is one of those angry ladies who are unfeminine, anti-family, and unreasonable. They claim that any man who is attracted to this kind of woman would have to be a wimp. But, let's face it, often the opposite point of view is equally uncharitable. An old style woman is defined as an object to be pitied, a doormat that breathes, submissive to a terrible man who is tyrannical at worst and merely selfish at best.

A more realistic and certainly less antagonistic description of how to tell old style from new is provided by sociologists John Scanzoni and Maximiliane Szinovacz. They give both groups full credit for wanting the best for both themselves and their families. The difference is in how each group defines what it means by "the best."

Scanzoni and Szinovacz point out that for generations—at least since the Industrial Revolution—what "the best" meant to *most* men and women was "making sure the man succeeds." The credo of the traditional woman goes something like this: "If he does well, we both do well; the whole family does well." Or put another way: "If I iron his shirts and he looks good, that's good enough for me."

What has changed, of course, is that women increasingly feel that what's best is that *both* man and woman should succeed. The credo of the modern woman is more like this: "He should do well, and I should do well, too." She is not saying that he, or the family as a whole, isn't important, but merely that she is an important part of the family.

As Scanzoni and Szinovacz describe her, a traditional woman who is offered a great job—but one that would interfere with her ability to get her husband's dinner on the table at 6:00 P.M., when he wants it—would turn the job down without a second thought. Why? Because she would *rather* have dinner on the table at six. She doesn't feel deprived, and she doesn't feel coerced. If taking that job means inconveniencing the man in her life, then it's too high a price to pay—like being offered a free week in Europe as long as you are willing to swim there. Thanks, but no thanks.

NEW STYLE, OLD STYLE

A traditional woman who is just a smidgen less cheerfully self-sacrificing might go so far as to broach the matter at home. Would he mind if she took the job? Would he allow her to? Would he be willing to eat at seven instead of six? However, if he says no, that just as surely ends the idea. The old style woman believes not only that the man is the boss, but also that he *should* be. She couldn't enjoy doing anything he disapproved of. And, of course, because she wouldn't think of him as Attila the Hun for being unwilling to delay his dinner hour in her behalf, he, quite naturally, wouldn't think of himself that way either.

The new style woman has a different outlook on life. She backs her man's goals, but not to the point of submerging herself in them. Thus, she would feel it is her right to consider this job. That doesn't mean she would automatically take it any more than it means she would automatically turn it down. But she would definitely expect to discuss the matter at home, and she would not so willingly take no for an answer. She would press her own position. If he objected, she would want to know why. She might even decide to take the job over his objections. But of course, since the new style woman values mutual trust, mutual respect, cooperation, and partnership, she would much prefer to reach some sort of compromise. And that could be anything. Maybe they would have dinner a little later. Maybe he could cook it, too.

It's pretty obvious, then, that if both halves of a couple are old style, a lot of matters that call for debate in other marriages don't even come up between them. Most "choices" are decided by custom or tradition. In the matter of household chores, for example, he is Mr. Outside (lawn mowing and car washing) and she is Mrs. Inside (dishes, diapers). Those choices still remaining (except for such homey matters as the color of the furniture) are decided by him. He takes for granted that any goals she has are secondary to his, and *she takes it for granted, too.* Thus, perfectly matched, they wonder why all others aren't as contented as *they* are.

Equally obvious, of course, is that when the new style woman is matched with a new style man, the combination works just as well, and they would say even better. He is proud of her for getting a job offer. He *wants* to do something to help. He, as well as she, assumes they can work something out. Under their roof, everything is fifty-fifty, nifty, nifty.

Alas, we are rarely so cleverly aligned.

And so we hear all the sad stories. There's the one about the new style man who left his old style woman behind. It turned out he didn't appreciate her willingness to live her life through him. Even though she cooked like Julia Child and wore her neckline down to here, he felt something was missing. She never understood his attitude. "But I did *everything* for him," she said.

More common are the tales of the determined modern woman who decides to give up on, rather than put up with, her rigidly traditional spouse. She doesn't appreciate his willingness to take total responsibility for her. She feels hemmed in. Though he looks like a movie star and bought her a mink, it isn't enough. He simply cannot understand it. "But I gave her *everything*," he moans.

Some years ago a man using the pen name Albert Martin wrote a piece for the *New York Times* that provides a typical example. Albert's marriage had broken up, and he was miserable about it. "I don't want to be [divorced]," he wrote. "I am horrified by the prospect. I think it is the most devastating thing that could happen to my family, but it is going to happen. My wife wants it." He went on to assure *Times* readers that he and his wife had led a wonderful life with "everything to live for." Their comfortable house, set on two acres with a woods, a ball field, and a toboggan slope, had been perfect for raising four boys. He had been happy, and he thought his wife was happy, too—until she told him she wanted a divorce.

"I am one man, hurt," he wrote, and predicted that many more men would be hurt—victimized by women whose concern for themselves was greater than their regard for "the needs of the family" or "of the other partner."

No doubt Albert thought his anguished words would bring sympathy for him and scorn for his ungrateful spouse. But no, most of the letters (from men as well as women) to the editor of the *Times* heaped the scorn on Albert for being an insensitive clod, a man so wrapped up in his own satisfactions that he neither knew nor cared what his wife thought. Letter after letter claimed to have Albert's number, all right, and it was zero.

Just recently, a similar appeal appeared in the *Philadelphia Inquirer*: "My marriage was splendid before my wife went to work. I could count on the meals being on time, the house clean and the children well taken care of. Now everything has changed. My wife says she's happy, but we're all going hungry, the house is a mess and the kids forever ask, 'Whatever happened to Mommy?' I don't know what's going to happen. What is a reasonable price for a family to pay for the wife's happiness?" Son of Albert. Albert Part

Two. Everything used to be splendid. For him, yes. For her, obviously not.

So many questions leap to mind. How frustrating to have only a few paragraphs and no way to get at the really juicy details. Has she truly abandoned her home and loved ones? We picture her out dancing until dawn—Margaret Trudeau at Studio 54 while hubby Pierre takes care of Canada and the kids. We picture her moving up in the corporation. "Just a second, B.G., while I tell my secretary to call my husband and tell him I'll be working late. Now, about our meeting next week in Cairo..." Could she be having an affair with B.G., too?

But also: Why is this family going hungry? Can they not open a can? Could it be they put down their forks rather than eat anything less than gourmet fare? Do they likewise refuse to eat if the meal is not "on time"? Why is the house such a mess? Can't *he* dust? Has he suggested hiring somebody to straighten up one afternoon a week?

Only one thing seems clear. Old style and new style are in conflict... again. What a mess.

What saves most of us, as I mentioned before, is that we are neither *totally* old style nor totally new but scattered erratically along a scale. Usually, she is closer to one, he closer to the other. Usually one is racing ahead while the other lags behind, yelling, "What's the hurry?"

Researchers have found that those who are younger and better educated are more likely to be new style, although it's hardly a guarantee. Better-educated men, in fact, seem to prefer the superwoman system: she has a career but cares for the house, too. Research also shows that the possibility for compromising between the old and the new increases the closer the partners are in job status, personal income, education, and self-esteem.

But they also found that, across the cultural and income spectrum, the gap between old and new is narrowing. More men are saying, for example, that they would be *willing* to do some household chores, even when they admit they are not doing them.

And it seems that even though the majority of Americans still claim the man is the head of house, that phrase no longer means quite what it used to. A guy may say, as a friend of mine did, "I've been pleading with my wife to take her hands out of the dishpan and do something she'd find more interesting, but she won't." If his wife were truly an old style wife, she would do what he says, even if what he says is new style. But, further, one could argue that she is being very new style by insisting on doing her own (old style) thing.

A woman may say, as a friend of mine did, "I used to wait on Walter hand and foot. But then, one Saturday morning, we were eating breakfast—which I had cooked and I had served—and he said, 'I don't have any jam.' And I said, 'It's on the second shelf of the refrigerator, on the left.' I think I was as surprised as he was that I didn't just jump up and get it. But when he saw that I wasn't moving, *he* got it. Heh. Heh. Heh."

She would claim that Walter is still head of the house, of course, but...

Small changes occur and are accepted—with puzzlement, perhaps, but with no great fuss. I interviewed a woman named Lila who recalled that shortly after she and her Jerry had returned from their honeymoon, they were sitting together in the living room and he said, "I'd like a glass of water." Whereupon she said, "So would I. Would you bring one for me when you get yours, hon?"

Well, that certainly was never what his mother said, so he said, "Can't you get it?" And she replied, "No more easily than you can. And it was your idea." At which point he got up, got two glasses of water, and said, "Here's yours."

Lila now ranks "Here's yours" in the same momentous league as Alexander Graham Bell's "Mr. Watson, come here; I want you" and Samuel F. B. Morse's "What hath God wrought?" All three sentences, she says, ushered in new eras of communication.

You might think that's no big deal. But Lila is right: what is today a minor change in a man-woman relationship would have been as unlikely as space flight for most women twenty-five years ago.

One interesting aspect of the changes now taking place is that we are not always aware of them as they happen. My friend Miriam claims that when she was first married, she considered it a point of pride that her husband could bring home friends for dinner unannounced anytime. She felt her ability to entertain on the spur of the moment proved what a good wife she was. Today, says Miriam, if her husband didn't call first, she'd be angry, because she doesn't want to be taken for granted. She has no idea when that change took place. It snuck in on her.

Not being aware of such changes can get couples into trouble. For example, every year he says, "I've decided I'm going to take my two weeks off in August." And every year she says, "Yes, dear." And then one day he says, "I've

NEW STYLE,
OLD STYLE

decided that this year we'll vacation on Mars." And she very indignantly retorts, "Maybe I don't want to go to Mars. Don't you think you should ask me how I feel about it?" And he says, "Huh? What's the matter with you?"

Being overly aware of change has its problems, too. Some ten years ago there were articles in popular women's magazines spelling out exactly what a modern relationship should be like. It was suggested that before the wedding, or maybe on the honeymoon, the twosome should sit down and write out a contract listing the rights and obligations of each. One such contract was published in *Redbook* magazine in 1971. This one had two sections. The first announced some admirable principles:

> The work that brings in more money is not more valuable;
> Each partner has an equal right to his/her own time, work, values, choices;
> Both parents must share all responsibility for care of children at home;
> Deviation from fifty-fifty sharing may call for revision of schedule.

The second part explained fully that fifty-fifty schedule— who would handle transportation of children, homework, sick care, cooking, shopping, cleaning, laundry, etc., etc., etc., and when.

It seems to me you could spend a lot of time arguing about whether something is fifty-fifty, particularly if it means all your schedules must be rearranged. It isn't an idea I favor. Besides, psychologist Mary Davenport claims it's impossible for any couple to reach fifty-fifty; even if they achieve it, each side will claim it feels like sixty-forty! She says, "If it feels like sixty-forty, you're lucky."

When all this contract talk was going around, Bernie said we definitely should have one, too, and immediately proposed a first clause that would assign all snow-shoveling duties to me. Needless to say, we never got around to the second clause. Yet the snow gets shoveled anyway. The matter has been resolved by such practical considerations as who is home when the snow stops, whether it is a one-shovel or two-shovel snow, which of us is occupied doing something more important, and who hides better.

The couples I know who claim to have, well, a sixty-forty relationship, say that it doesn't mean doing every single thing by halves. It doesn't mean you make every decision together. It depends on what your interests are. It depends on what you consider important. Some things will naturally be decided by him, some by you, and you only have to fight about the rest.

When I asked my women friends what would indicate to them that a man was new style, they all agreed he would have to show some recognition of their needs. Yet no two cries for simple justice were alike. One woman said that her husband ("just like a man") doesn't clean the bathroom until it's totally covered with mold and she herself is turning green. If he were new style, she said, he wouldn't wait around to be told. But another woman found that kind of goal downright unbelievable: "You know a man who would actually consent to clean a bathroom and you're *complaining*?

NEW STYLE, OLD STYLE

Mona says she'd call it even if her husband just showed a little appreciation, but Nan says she wants more than appreciation; she wants cooperation.

Rita asks, "How come *he* can announce he's going on a fishing trip and expect me to go along with the idea though not on the trip, but if I were to announce that I was going off for a week and he could look after the kids and wait for the electrician, he'd go into shock?" And Sandy flatly states that, since they have now moved four times so that he can get a promotion, it's his turn to move now so that she can get ahead.

In short, what you want, what would satisfy you, and whether you get it depend on where you and your man are on the old style–new style continuum—more specifically, how far apart you are from each other.

It's terrible to admit this, but even those of us who believe in change can have mixed emotions about it. On the one hand, when I tell Bernie I have a meeting to go to and I won't be home for dinner, I know I wouldn't like it at all if he put his foot down and told me that my job is to cook. On the other hand, I'm not as thrilled as I might be at how wonderfully he manages without me. "You *could* look just a little more desolate," I have told him. "A brief speech about indigestion wouldn't go amiss."

Sometimes when the men decide to enlist in our new style ways, we'd just as soon they did not. I don't want Bernie to learn to cook, for example, because I like to cook and I like things in the kitchen done my way. If that makes me a throwback, so be it.

Miriam says Milton volunteered, without being asked, to accompany her to the supermarket, to push the cart, and to help make selections. But after a few trips in which he compared products in one aisle when she wanted to move ahead, and she compared prices in another aisle while he grew impatient, she decided she'd rather he stayed home to carry in the bags when she got there.

What rapidly becomes clear is that in this business of how two lovers become friends there is no right or wrong way. It is, as lawyers would put it, whatever pleases the parties at any given time.

I don't think I could ever have imagined in advance the kinds of choices that have come up. There was the time that Bernie thought we should buy a new sofa, and I wanted to spend the money on a copying machine. I thought that showed how modern we had become. Wouldn't you think the woman would want the sofa, the man would want the machine? Apparently, we hadn't changed that much because we got the sofa first. We weren't exactly old style either, because it was understood that the very next big purchase would be my copier—which he uses more than I do, as it happens. But, then, I sit on his couch.

It seems to me that all we are asking of men is that they move closer to where we are. She doesn't have to prove that his way is inferior or accept that hers is. If he says Mother Nature intended males to be in charge and then brings up birds, she can bring up bees. There is more than one way of doing things, that's all.

We aren't asking that men approve of where women are going, just that they accept us as we accept them. This is a kind of variation on the golden rule: do unto others as they would like done unto them, even if you think it's nuts.

NEW STYLE, OLD STYLE

Whenever I get into a discussion of new style relationships at a party, inevitably a man raises the question of whether these new roles for men and women are good or bad, right or wrong. That kind of debate is interesting but basically meaningless. It's like arguing whether we were all better off before television. Even if you agree, do you plan to throw out your set? If we had a coal-burning furnace as my parents did when I was growing up, I know Bernie and I would get a lot of exercise shoveling coal and hauling ashes. Possibly we would be much healthier. Yet we haven't ordered one. A case can be made that I would save money if I washed the dishes by hand, but the fact of the matter is that when my dishwasher has a breakdown, so do I.

My friend Arthur, when I tell him I am writing about new style women (he being an old style man and proud of it), says, "Oh, I don't know. Men won't be as happy. And I'm not sure women will be happy either."

I try to tell him that we just can't talk about this kind of change in that way. Were people happier before the invention of the car or the computer? Who knows? Once you have driven a distance in ten minutes that used to take an hour, or once you have withdrawn money from a bank machine at ten o'clock at night, you realize that you not only can't go back in time, but don't want to. And woe to the wicked soul who tries to take these new pleasures away.

A guy who is more old style than new may think a woman who is more new style than old is just plain crazy. That's okay. The question is, will he do something crazy for this crazy woman who is so crazy about him?

Really now, how can he resist?

4

THE NEW GUILT

It is axiomatic that as soon as some new social trend sweeps America, a new disease develops to go with it. And so we have seen the emergence of tennis player's elbow, video game thumb, quiche eater's indigestion, and, of course, new style woman's guilt.

This last is characterized by the terrible feeling that you are not living up to what is expected of you. It's ridiculous, but it's common. I know why it happens, too.

For at least the past ten years, women have been engaged in a struggle to convince *themselves* as well as their men that it is okay and not crazy to want to have a separate identity, that it's okay and not decadent to want to do something besides (or in addition to) caring for house and children, that it's okay and not bitchy to want a man to return some of the care they give him.

That the women's movement has succeeded is indicated by this change of opinion: in 1972 the majority of Americans, including the majority of women, opposed the notion of equality for women; by 1982, however, a majority of both men and women favored the idea.

Here's the problem. There have been so many books, articles, speeches, and such on this subject that sometimes we confuse what we *should be able to do* with what we should do. We confuse what we think we want with what we think we *should* want, and we end up feeling just terrible about it.

A high-powered female editor was married to a man who, she boasted widely, was new style right down to his very nonthreatened, share-and-share-alike, double-bed-but separate-checkbooks soul. And was *she* new style? Ha. Would you like to see the suit she filed with the Equal Employment Opportunity Commission?

However, this poor woman, who might seem to be the very epitome of modern womanhood, suffered a crisis of conscience when she had a child.

Both she and her husband wanted this child. There was no doubt in either her mind or his that he would stand diaper duty and get up his share of times in the middle of the night. The problem was that she wanted to quit her job and stay home with the baby. She *wanted* to do more than he.

When she first got pregnant she assured everyone at work that of course she would return as soon as her maternity leave was up. When that time came, however, she asked for an extension of the leave, pleading housekeeper problems. Finally she faced up to the truth she had not wanted to admit: she didn't want to come back.

She met her female colleagues for lunch and shamefacedly confessed. She was embarrassed. She felt she'd let them down. She feared that when word got out that she actually wanted to do something so old-fashioned as staying home with a baby, she would be stripped of her new style epaulets and drummed out of the corps.

"It's all right," we assured her. "The revolution has

been fought to open new options, not to eliminate any of the old ones."

I could well understand her confusion, having been through the same sort of thing myself, although in another context, several years before.

I was writing a column in a newspaper. There were two columnists on this newspaper at the time, one female (me) and one male (Joe McGinness, who later became nationally known for his book *The Selling of the President*). I was writing on subjects, politics and such, that women rarely got a chance to comment on in the late sixties, and I was very much aware of it. Too aware, as it turned out.

One day the newspaper announced that McGinness was being sent to Vietnam and would write dispatches from there. My phone began to ring. Women callers wanted to know why I wasn't going to Vietnam along with or even instead of Joe. "They can't do this to you," they said. "You should sue. They are overlooking you only because you are a woman. Did those editors think that only a man could cover a war? Those ignorant bums. Those narrow-minded wretches." And so forth.

By the time I got home that night, I was a wreck. I felt put down, done in, and discarded. I sobbed as I described to Bernie the terrible wrong I had suffered. "He is being sent to Vietnam," I sniffled. "And they didn't ask me."

"I didn't know you wanted to go to Vietnam," Bernie said. "You've never mentioned it."

"I don't," I said. Sob.

And he said, "But if what you are not getting is only what you don't want anyway, why are you crying?"

I had to think that one over.

"Whose life do you want to live," Bernie asked, giving me even more to think about, "Yours or Joe's?"

In truth, all I was really concerned about was that others, who, if they were in my place would have wanted to go, should not feel I was letting them down. But I couldn't live their lives either.

Would the paper have sent me to Vietnam if I had wanted to go? I'll never know. My guess is, probably not. But since I had decided that not getting what I didn't want was not the worst thing that could happen to me, I ceased to care.

Although I admit I wouldn't have minded letting the world *know* I didn't care. Unfortunately, there is never a good way to do that. I think it would be nice if we could walk down the street wearing signs that read "It isn't true what you heard; it was all a misunderstanding" or "I didn't want it anyway." People who aren't thinking what we think they're thinking would be puzzled, of course, but at least for everybody else the record would be set straight.

Anyway, because new style is so new, there is a lot of this kind of confusion around. At a meeting of a women's organization a while ago, I happened to mention that I thought Bernie was very new style. I was challenged on this from the floor.

"Does he wash dishes?" one of the members asked.

"We have an automatic dishwasher," I replied.

She was too smart to fall for that. "Let me put it this way," she said. "Who takes the dishes out and puts them away?"

She had me there. "I do."

THE NEW GUILT

"You call *that* new style?"
General derision. "Booooo."
"Hisss."
"Give our regards to Queen Victoria!"

Only later did I think of what I should have said. I should have told them that, even though I know the matter of sharing chores and child-rearing duties looms large in many households, it is not a priority in mine and I don't feel bad about that. The situation in every household is different.

What is very important to me is being a participant in decisions that affect both of us and having the freedom to make decisions that affect my career. I want to be encouraged. I want support. If I have to go someplace at night for an interview, I think Bernie should understand that that's important. And he does, too.

When I'm facing a deadline and still typing away at 8:00 P.M., he'll know that what I'm doing is more vital than dinner. If I need supplies, he will forage for me. If I am stuck for an idea and wake up at 3:00 A.M., tossing and turning because some article is just not working out, he will wake up and talk it over with me until the problem is solved. Once it is, I immediately fall asleep again, and he has insomnia for the rest of the night. No system is perfect.

I might add that I don't feel guilty about keeping Bernie up this way, and don't think I should. After all, it doesn't happen every night. He is in no danger of turning into a zombie from lack of sleep. For another, I would do the same—or the equivalent—for him, and he knows that.

Most important, I don't think it is right to feel guilty

when a man willingly does something you'd like even though it is inconvenient for him, because you then rob him of the full *pleasure* of doing it.

I'll explain. The fact that the new style woman no longer lives totally to serve her man doesn't mean she can't enjoy doing things to please him. Making him happy still gives her a kick, after all. Well, why not assume, then, that a man will enjoy doing things to please the woman he loves, too. You can bet Bernie knows I'm pleased.

O. Henry's wonderful story "The Gift of the Magi" makes just this point. An impoverished couple give each other Christmas gifts. She cuts and sells her beautiful long hair to get enough money to buy him a fob for his treasured pocket watch. He sells the pocket watch to get enough money to buy her a comb for her beautiful long hair.

I cry every time I read it.

At this point, you may well be saying, as my challengers at that women's organization did, "Enough of this diversion, just what do you do about housework?"

Not much. Which brings me to still another category of new style woman's guilt, middle-class division.

What *we* do is hire somebody to come in once a week to do the basic dusting and sweeping for *us*. That still leaves plenty of daily chores, of which he does some and I do most. Still, most of the major stuff is done by a pro who apologizes to no one for knowing her trade as well as any mechanic, bricklayer, accountant, or psychologist knows his or hers.

Now, there are those who would like to make a woman feel guilty for hiring another woman as a housekeeper. Here, for example, is the first sentence of a column by Art Buch-

THE NEW GUILT

wald: "Behind every liberated woman, there is another woman who has to do the dirty work for her."

Does that sound friendly to you? This piece goes on to tell the story of an attorney who says she could not pursue her career if it weren't for Juanita who "takes care of the house and the children and cooks our meals." The attorney's husband, Buchwald notes, refuses to pitch in.

At one point Art comments, "it seems ironic that in order to be free a woman must find another slave to replace her."

C'mon, hold it just a minute, now. It's true that it is easier to have a job outside the home if someone else does — or helps with — the jobs inside the home. Somebody has to do the housework. But there is nothing "ironic" about that and nothing wrong with it.

I write stories for editors who used to write but who don't want to anymore. Big deal. They don't say this sort of thing where men are concerned, do they? If a man is a carpenter and then becomes a building contractor who hires other carpenters to do what he used to, do people dump on him? Do they say: Humph. Look at him. He hired someone else to do his job for him. Do people look down their noses at the carpenters who work for him? No, they do not.

Nobody knocks Bernie when *he* hires help. And he does. I know women whose husbands have repaired every appliance in the kitchen four times. I know men who have rewired the basement, retiled the roof, and added an entire new wing to the house. My guy is not among them. Bernie's idea of do-it-yourself is dialing the plumber's number.

I know many new style women who buy the idea that they should feel guilty if they hire an outside expert to clean or care for children—even if the housekeeper *likes* to clean, even if the children are cared for by a day care center that employs a Ph.D. in child development and a world-renowned specialist in sibling rivalry.

But not me. I got over that some time ago. I don't feel guilty about becoming an employer. Bernie doesn't either. Our position is that although you might become upset if you hire someone who burns the house down or teaches the children how to pick pockets, hiring in and of itself is legitimate. Whether hiring someone is a solution for you depends on your need and/or your budget and also on whether someone applies for the job. You need feel guilty about hiring someone only if you don't pay a decent wage. And that is true of any employer.

I realize that my choices and my systems may not work for others. But what others arrange or think important may not work for me, either. There is no point in feeling pressured about it. It is tough enough, heaven knows, to work out partnership arrangements when both of you know what you want—particularly when what you want is already more than he wants to give—without complicating matters with what you think you *should* want, what *others* want, and what others *say* you should want.

Good grief. Half the time I don't even know what I want. I know that I want to be my own woman. I know I want to stand on my own two feet where my career is concerned, and yet... there are times when a crucial choice haunts me and I long for the good old days when the man of the house told the woman of the house exactly what to do.

THE NEW GUILT

"I can't make up my mind," I say to Bernie. "Tell me what I should say." And he replies, "It's your problem. You're the one who has to live with it. I'll be happy to talk it over with you, but the decision is up to you."

Curses. This is bad news for somebody who doesn't like feeling guilty. "But what if it goes wrong?" I wail miserably. "Who will I have to *blame*?"

5

WHO WAS THAT MASKED MAN?

There are times when you feel you just don't recognize him anymore. There are times when you say to yourself, Who is this impostor pretending to be the fellow who usually lives here? Who kidnapped the guy I fell in love with and replaced him with this substandard brand?

He buries himself in a newspaper and doesn't seem to hear what you say. He criticizes a dish you fussed over for hours. He suddenly snaps, "Because I say so, that's why."

"Humph," you sniff. "He wasn't like this when we met."

How true. They never are.

You find yourself asking, Did I misjudge him when we met? Did he lie to me when we were going together? Has he changed? Have I?

And probably all the answers are yes.

It is a rare couple who truly know each other when they make the commitment to marry and/or live together and an even rarer couple who realize it. Sure, we tend to view a lot more bare skin in advance than our grandmothers did, if we believe what they say, but the terrible truth is we still play the same kind of courtship games that the Victorians raised to an art form. We put up fronts. We play our roles. We don't want to scare a good prospect away. Both sides do it, too.

Humorist Judith Viorst wrote, "All the time I was letting him borrow my comb and hang up his wet raincoat in my closet, I was really waiting to stop letting him. And... all the time he was saying how he loved my chicken pot pie, he was really waiting to stop eating it."

How familiar that sounds. When I met Bernie, I made him a tuna-fish sandwich on white bread. He praised it lavishly. He asked for seconds. I glowed. It was only later that I learned he hates white bread. He hasn't eaten a slice since. When we were going together, we used to go bike riding at dawn on Sunday mornings. "How wonderful," I said to him then. "How romantic." But now I can't remember the last time we did that because I'd really rather sleep.

That's how it goes. We keep our tempers in check. We keep our bad habits in hiding—to the extent we realize they are bad habits. He says what his first wife did that annoyed him, but not what he did that annoyed her. She's had experience; she pretends she's a virgin. He's a virgin but pretends he has experience.

Even when we recognize faults or drawbacks, we try to ignore or minimize them because we are concentrating on something much more important—getting each other.

We pretend to love all his friends, his family, and his hobbies, not to mention his habit of watching football for *fourteen straight hours on Thanksgiving*. He fakes it, too, although—let's face it—not as much.

This goes on longer than you might think. I know a couple who lived together for years before they were married. They thought there could be no more surprises for them. They knew each other so well. Wrong. She knew he was an early riser and rolled the toothpaste from the bottom. He knew she liked to cook. But they both concede that they learned much more after marriage. The mere fact of legal, total, and permanent commitment brought out sides of their characters that were either not revealed or not observed before. As he put it, "Finally we could just relax and be rotten."

Not only do we fool each other but we sometimes fool ourselves as well. Psychiatrist Clifford Sager has written about what he calls the "unwritten marriage contract." He claims that, almost without exception, each partner walks down the aisle with an agreement in his or her brain—each one assuming that the other has accepted it in every little detail.

Suppose a woman thinks a man should call if he's going to be late for dinner. In her head, her groom has agreed to do this every time. The man, however, thinks that if he mentions in the morning that he might be late, there is no need for anything more. In *his* head, his bride thinks that, too.

Now, they never ever talked of this while they were courting. He promised to climb every mountain and swim every river, but the subject of telephoning never came up. However, when he doesn't call, she feels he has "broken his word," and she is plenty upset. He, in turn, is annoyed because, after all, she "knows the score." Oh, dear.

Marriage counselor Mary Davenport says that the coming together of two families can be like the merger of two kingdoms with separate customs, treasuries, and standing armies. If she has taken it for granted they'll do things the way her family does, while he is busy taking it for granted that things will go the way he is used to, watch out!

His family always sends birthday cards. Her family doesn't bother, so she doesn't send his mother a birthday card. Now he thinks she doesn't like his mother. Her family believes in arguing quietly; voices are never raised in anger. His family comes from a more emotional tradition; now and then they enjoy a good scream. When he yells at her, she "knows it's all over" because "no man treats a woman he loves like that."

In ways big and little, important or un-, this kind of misunderstanding occurs. We see what we want to see. We believe what we want to believe. Sometimes we're wrong.

In his book *My Life in Court*, attorney Louis Nizer tells of a couple who went for long walks when they were courting. When they grew tired, they'd sit down on a bench, and he would take off her shoes and rub her feet. She thought this was sooooo loving, so caring, so sweet. Only after the wedding did she discover that rubbing her feet was *all* he wanted to do. She'd married a foot fetishist.

But, it also happens, even when we read our partner correctly, that the qualities that most appeal to us while we're being wooed are those that most annoy us later.

Consider the sad saga of Sally who fell for a man of few words. She was impressed by his strong, silent sexiness. "He doesn't need words," she sighed. "He is a man of action. His kiss tells me all I want to know." But after they married, his kiss wasn't nearly as informative as she had thought. Nor as frequent, if the truth be known. Now she spends a

WHO WAS THAT MASKED MAN?

lot of time complaining that he never talks to her. He is too bottled up. He shuts her out. And so forth.

Or how about Hannah, who was so thrilled with her beloved's articulate style? "He's so glib, so witty, so interesting," she bragged. "I hang on his every syllable. I could listen to him forever." After a few months in close quarters, she thinks forever may be more than she can stand. Now she complains that all he wants to do is hear himself talk. "He isn't interested in anything I have to say. He doesn't know how to listen," she laments. Oh, woe.

Nell fell for Mel because he was so ambitious. She knew he'd be successful. She was sure that someday he would have money and influence and prestige. And she was right, too. The guy is flying high. He is also flying often. As a rising young executive, Mel is frequently away on business trips, and Nell is left alone. He works long hours at the office. She sits long hours watching TV. Now *her* ambition is that he lose some of his.

Lil went for Phil because he was a take-charge guy. You know the type. She admired a man who could make up his mind... and her mind, too. When they were dating, he would ask, "Anyplace special you'd like to go?" And she would bat her eyelashes in time-honored style, breathe heavily, and say, "Anywhere you want to go is special to me." Now she complains that he always expects to get his way. But she wants more say. Uh-oh.

I'm sure you get the idea.

Usually, of course, we don't change our minds *completely* about those qualities we found appealing. It's just that we would like them modified a bit. Or we would like them to go away at certain times or in particular situations. I always believed that one of Bernie's most admirable characteristics was the way he stood his ground and fought for those things he thinks are right. I still think that's admirable, unless, of course, I feel he is wrong about what's right. And then I claim he is being unduly stubborn if not downright unreasonable.

Anyway, given all the ways that two people can misunderstand each other, it is truly a miracle that so many of us manage even as well as we do. Some have said that's only because women simply give up and give in, but I think that's overstating the case.

Usually, as two people live together, they both make adjustments, whether or not they want to or even realize they are doing so. The need to change may come with the passage of time, with a job change, with children, with illness, with sudden riches or fame. It can come—and this is what concerns us here—through changes in the society we live in and in the mental set of half its population. Suddenly, not only is he no longer the fellow you thought he was, but he is having the same thoughts about you. You thought you got Superman, and you ended up with Clark Kent. And here he was, perfectly satisfied with Diana Prince, and now he's got Wonder Woman. "Great Hera!" as W.W. would say.

This can cause a romance to founder. There is no getting away from that. It is entirely possible that once two intelligent people come to a complete and deep understanding of exactly where the other stands on everything, they may *not* live happily ever after. Once he understands perfectly what she wants and she understands with total clarity what he wants, one or the other (or both) may cry, "Who needs this?"

To wit:

"My idea of a proper wife is a woman who keeps her mouth shut and walks ten paces behind me."

"My idea of your idea is unprintable."

Or:

"I have decided to move to a Pacific island where the mail boat calls only once a year so that I can try my hand at raising coconuts and inventing a new religion."

"'Bye."

We all know the story of Rumpelstiltskin, in which the miller's daughter gets to marry the king because the miller has told the king she can spin flax into gold. A typical courtship story since it turns out she can't deliver. This king, apparently not believing in divorce, tells his bride that if she doesn't deliver the goods, she dies.

According to the story, she is rescued by a little man who does have gold-spinning talent. The first time this happens, the little man accepts payment of a ribbon. The second time he takes a ring the king has given her. The third time the gold-spinner demands her firstborn child as payment, unless she can successfully guess his name. She does—it's Rumpelstiltskin, of course—and that makes the little man so angry, he quite literally splits in half.

As far as the Brothers Grimm were concerned, that was the end of the story. But it couldn't be. The king who married because he wanted flax spun into gold and got it three times running will want a fourth delivery. And then what?

We don't want to tell little children about this, but the queen is in big trouble. The fact that the king understands perfectly that the queen can't make gold and never could will probably not save that relationship or the queen.

But, thank goodness, this is not the usual situation. Much more common are the situations in which a couple's misunderstanding of each other's expectations leads to hurt and anger that neither side wants. Each one feels that he or she would be happier if only the other partner would be more reasonable, and each one has a different definition of what "reasonable" means.

Sometimes what seems to be an enormous problem between two people can dissolve if only they can find a way to let each other know the bargain they think has been made. Psychiatrist Aaron Beck tells the story of a couple who almost called off their marriage because they so totally misread each other's motives. She had a cold and asked him to stay home from an evening meeting to be with her. He said the meeting was too important to miss. She sulked. If he wouldn't even stay home when she had a cold, she concluded, then she certainly could not count on him if anything important ever happened. Meanwhile, he fumed. If she was going to ask him to stay home for a lousy cold, he'd never be able to get out of the house. In other words, while she was busy feeling rejected, he was feeling trapped.

Lucky for them, they were both friends of Beck's and they told him separately of their complaint. He advised them to compare notes.

WHO WAS THAT MASKED MAN?

After that, it was simple, says Beck. The meeting-goer promised that if something serious ever happened, he'd be there. The cold-sufferer promised not to chain him to the front steps. This is an agreement both can probably live up to because they know it exists.

Often we can live with change if we simply acknowledge that there *is* change. If he discovers that she does not adore football, he can probably cope with that as long as she lets him know she's still willing to put up with his fixation. If she wants him to help her in the house, he may do so if she puts it to him as something she didn't expect before but would like now—as opposed to something he was supposed to have been doing before and fouled up.

Which brings us once again to the differences between the old style and new style ways of life.

New style women (and men) tend to think in terms of what is "fair." Generally, she has decided that if she has to defer to him in almost everything and he rarely defers to her, that's not fair. Old style men (and women) tend to think in terms of "what's expected." Generally, he believes that if he works hard and is loyal, she should do her duty, too. Mixing these two sets of values leads to conflict and frustration, both of which are only made worse if those involved do not realize what is going on.

Thus if she thinks that he "knows what is fair" but refuses to cooperate, she may think he is being deliberately mean or that he doesn't love her anymore. If he thinks that she knows "what's expected" but won't do her part, he may think she is just being bitchy and doesn't respect him anymore.

You might think this kind of mix-up is unlikely because women *know* that men do not think as women do. I'm not so sure. I think most of us tend to think that others at least *know* what's right even if they don't *do* it, and that's not the same thing. In this area of male-female thinking, I believe we tend to fool each other quite a bit.

Sometimes a woman will pretend to be more traditional than she is when she is being courted. She doesn't want to frighten him away. Meanwhile, he is working under a phony new style cover. He tells her he "wouldn't hesitate at all to vote for a woman for president." How is she supposed to know he also thinks a female chief executive should clean up after White House banquets?

Sometimes she truly *was* traditional when they got together. Now she has changed, and he is shocked. Or he doesn't seem to notice that she has changed and *she* is shocked.

In other words, if she thinks he is reneging on a deal he doesn't know he's made, she may blast him with "I have to do double work while you sit on your duff reading a paper as if this house doesn't concern you." Which causes him to be defensive and snarl, "It happens that I work very hard and you don't mind spending the money I make and how come you had to *invite your mother to visit* on the weekend you know *damn well* I want to go to the fishing tournament?"

On the other hand, if she views him as someone who had a different contract in his head because he has a different value structure—let me put it this way: she sees him as a person in need of rehabilitation, someone who is culturally deprived, an alien recently arrived from Pluto—she is more likely to approach this matter with diplomatic skill.

She might simply say, "Honey, sorry to bother you, but I badly need your help. Would you pick up Junior's toys and put him to bed while I finish up here? Then we can both relax together."

He might not do it, but I've found that this kind of offer is hard to refuse. This may not wholly satisfy a woman's need for total equality, but she can console herself with the thought that the essence of diplomacy, wherever it is practiced, is compromise.

In short, it is all too easy to have a misunderstanding. With a little understanding, however, it is harder to miss.

6

MAKING THINGS WORSE THAN THEY ARE

There is nothing so bad, I always say, that it cannot be made worse than it is just by thinking it's worse than it is. This is a trick that requires no outside help. All we need is us.

I bring this up because, even though I claim that there are things I do right in this matter of having a new style relationship, I sometimes think that I am helped even more by what I don't do wrong. Or don't do very often, anyway.

I don't think up things to get upset about, for example. I have been told this shows a lack of imagination, but I don't care.

Some people I know are forever looking for *meanings* in everything that happens. If he leaves an apple on the table, she worries for hours whether he is trying to tell her that they have to move to New York or that he wants to buy a computer. To me, an apple is just a piece of fruit until I'm told otherwise.

Even if something is obviously wrong, I don't leap to believe the worst. If we get a bill that is obviously an overcharge, I'll assume a typing error and call to get it corrected before I threaten to sue. And usually that's all I have to do. If Bernie were ever missing for hours, I would not torment myself with visions of him having an affair. Rather, I would imagine him captured by pirates, lost in a snowstorm, stranded in a ditch. I look at it this way: if you are going to insist on inventing events that you don't know to be true, you might as well be upbeat about it.

Life certainly hands us enough real problems without our having to invent or imagine more. I've always felt I don't have to go looking for trouble because it does such a good job of looking for me. If and when you have health or money problems, when the roof leaks, the furnace has just blown up, the children have the flu, and you find out he *is* having an affair, you will have ample opportunity then to be anxious and hysterical. My policy is really very simple: I don't believe the worst until it has happened. And since very often the worst *doesn't* happen (bad, maybe, but not the worst), I am saved a lot of grief.

But probably the best thing I *don't* do (very much, anyway) is to believe that I am personally responsible for everything that goes wrong. I think that particular attitude is a common affliction of women. Who was it who said that if you ask a man where a steak came from, he will say, "The supermarket," but if you ask a woman, she will say, "Why? What's the matter with it?"

If he puts down her pasta, she feels she's been put down, too. If she buys a lamp and asks, "What do you think?" and he thinks it should go back to the store, she'll see the light dimming on their love affair. If he is in a bad mood, she will automatically assume that she caused it or, at the very least, failed in her duty to deflect it.

I can understand this. After all, we women have been told for thousands of years—and for most of those years we believed it—that it is up to us to make our man happy, to

MAKING THINGS WORSE THAN THEY ARE

clear his path, to support his every need. And so, naturally, when the man is unhappy, when his path appears cluttered, when we can't even figure out what his need is, we conclude that we have failed him. And we naturally assume that he, too, thinks we have failed him.

My friend Miriam calls this the kiss-and-make-better complex, after what mothers tell children with skinned knees: "Come here. Mommy will kiss it and make it better." We seem to feel we should be able to do that with every form of skinned knee life can provide, even though it's impossible.

As a self-proclaimed new style woman, I feel entitled to chuck this kind of thinking. For example, if Bernie comes home and isn't smiling and isn't much in the mood for talking, either, except to comment at dinner that "this chicken is pretty bland," I deduce from this that something is wrong either with him or with the chicken. I don't immediately conclude that something must be wrong with me.

I am the first to admit that if Bernie never liked *anything* I cooked or bought or did, I wouldn't see much reason to like *him*. We all need appreciation and encouragement. Yes, there is much to be said for common courtesy and tact. I realize it's been proven scientifically that total honesty and openness is a curse. And we all know there are times when it is much better to exclaim "I love it, it's just what I wanted" about a gift that really would be much more useful in undermining the morale of enemy troops.

But the fact that we all need approval and that we desire some humane lying now and again is not the same thing as interpreting any negative comment as a personal attack.

I admit it is often difficult *not* to take grouchy behavior personally, particularly when there are only two of you in the room. I mean, he may be grumbling at the whole world, but when you look around all you see is you.

Clearly, it does not help that people often do divert their anger from somebody they can't yell at to somebody more convenient. Like yelling at the waitress when you can't get at the chef. Like yelling at the children when you're mad at yourself. The one who gets it may simply be last in line. The big boss yells at the manager who yells at the supervisor who takes it out on the salesman who goes home and says the spaghetti tastes burned. If this were a fair world, the spaghetti cooker would complete the circle by dumping the whole pot on the big boss's head. But we rarely get such satisfaction.

At best, what we get the opportunity to do, if we take it, is to step back from the scene and say, "I wonder what's eating him?" (Or "What are we eating?" as the case may be.) I tell myself with some frequency that *everything that upsets my family is not my doing!* It helps. If Bernie is grumpy, I don't rush to blame myself for his behavior. I concentrate first on other lesser explanations, such as: he has just discovered that our house is about to be sold at sheriff's sale, or he has lost his wallet, or the car was stolen. He just hasn't gotten around to telling me yet.

With similar objectivity, I consider the possibility that his comment about the chicken does not mean he is dissatisfied with our life together or even with my ability as a chef. It may mean only that this particular dish needs more seasoning. Which means all I have to do is look for a salt shaker as opposed to a bridge to jump off.

MAKING THINGS WORSE
THAN THEY ARE

The reason such objectivity is so helpful, I have found, is because usually the next step to feeling that your personal work is being given demerits is to get angry at the one you think is handing them out.

It's like this. Let us say the stores are out of his favorite cereal. He'll have to make do with a less crunchy brand. He naturally isn't happy about this. She is not happy either because she feels she has failed him by not bringing home the right box. Any true helpmate would have searched the next six counties at least. First she thinks this. Then she thinks—given his disappointed expression—that *he* thinks this. At which point she thinks, Does he think I have nothing else to do but shop for cereal?

Obviously, there is much too much thinking going on here.

And this is not a problem that an old style man is causing this woman; this is a problem a woman can only cause for herself. First she adopts an old style attitude about feeling guilty if she doesn't fill his every moment with bliss, and then she becomes resentful, as only a new style woman can do, at the very idea that this should be expected of her. You may say that a true new style woman would not suffer such confusion. All I can say is: sometimes I do.

But I fight it, and you should, too.

7

GETTING HIS ATTENTION

The story is told of a farmer who had a mule that could dance and leap and count with his hoof and do many other such fancy tricks. The farmer claimed he could convince the mule to do just about anything he asked merely by making a gentle request and patting the mule on the head. People were astounded at this, of course, because mules are notorious for doing only what they want to—usually nothing—and no more.

"But if your mule is so cooperative," one skeptic inquired, "why are you carrying that two-by-four?"

"Oh, that," the farmer replied. "That's just to get his attention."

Indeed.

Many women claim that the man they love can be "stubborn as a mule" when it comes to hearing what they are saying, and they wish they knew a sure way—short of slugging him with a two-by-four, that is—to "get his attention." This can be a very big problem.

In the first episode of the TV series "Seven Brides for Seven Brothers," a bride discovers that the home she is to share with her new husband must also be shared with his six younger brothers, who are none too pleased to have a female in their midst. They let her know this by ignoring her. At the dinner table, they don't even pass the serving dishes her way. When she asks, "Can I say something?" no one—including the groom—seems to hear her.

Finally, without a further word, she stands up, smiles sweetly, and turns the table over. Plates of food splatter; chairs tumble. The fellows are surprised. "I will not be ignored, and I will not starve to death," she announces calmly.

"You've got my attention," one of brothers calls from the floor.

"Women are doing all kinds of things to get men's attention today," says Psychiatrist Walter Brackelmanns, "getting divorces, having affairs, screaming, turning off the television set."

Last year fifteen young women in Smithfield, Rhode Island, got not only their husbands' attention but also, it seems, the attention of half the population of the free world when they launched a housewives' strike. They formed a picket line and proclaimed their intention not to cook, clean, or cuddle until their demands were met.

The demands were modest enough: all they wanted from their men was some conversation and appreciation. As one of the wives put it, "A mother's day goes twenty-four hours with no thank you, no affection, and the husband comes home and lies on the couch. There's nothing there."

When reporters called from all over the United States and as far away as Denmark and Germany to get the men's reaction, the husbands promptly proved themselves to be everything their wives were complaining about. Said one, "She's just griping because I don't pay enough attention to her." Just? Said another, "I didn't put a gun to her head and force her to get married."

GETTING HIS ATTENTION

The husbands objected to the strike, of course, but they could hardly ignore it. And after three days of embarrassing publicity, they grudgingly agreed to consider their wives' demands. One husband even publicly admitted that maybe he'd "fallen short in some ways."

The Rhode Island wives said they were happy the strike had been settled, but they were saving their picket signs just in case. "It's easy to say yes, yes, yes to us when you want to get off the national news," said one, "but if we don't see some action, we're walking out again."

Quite clearly, in some households, merely letting a guy know a problem exists isn't enough.

A woman who wrote to newspaper columnist Ann Landers said she had complained bitterly to her husband about his habit of taking pictures of her in the nude. He carried said pictures around with him in his wallet, and she didn't like it. But he paid no attention to her objections, she reported, until the day she bought a camera and began taking pictures of *him* in the nude.

"He didn't realize how out of shape he had gotten," she wrote. "After two photo sessions, he offered to make a deal—he'd stop making candids if I would." Ann Landers approved.

Marriage counselor Sally Green tells of a woman who, with some frequency, would take off every stitch of clothing, not to pose for a picture but to run naked down the street. That caused her shocked and embarrassed husband to jump up and run after her with a coat. Finally, both of them came to see Mrs. Green for help. She suggested that, as a start, they try to think of easier ways for her to get his attention.

You get the idea. It is a basic fact of life that you cannot convince another—male or female—to see things your way if you don't first get his or her attention. The trick is to do this without damage to either party.

Unfortunately, some of the age-old techniques we have employed to hit men over the head seem to raise more bumps on our skulls than on theirs. During the very messy custody trial between Roxanne and Peter Pulitzer, the publishing heir, one of her friends testified that the only reason Roxanne had all those affairs her husband accused her of having was "to make him jealous." Presumably so that he would then pay more attention to her. If that, indeed, was the case, Peter didn't get the message. What he got, instead, was a divorce, both kids, and continued possession of his money.

So often, such standard attention-getters as screaming and breaking dishes result only in laryngitis and another mess to clean up. Some people feel that yelling is an aid to understanding. You know, like the traveler who doesn't speak the native language and so turns up the volume in English: "WHERE IS THE EIFFEL TOWER? THE TOWER. WHERE IS IT?" But my feeling is that screaming and dish-breaking work well only when resorted to as last-ditch measures in case of dire emergency. One might call this the "burglar alarm principle." That is, if an alarm sounds only when a burglar is climbing through the window, the neighbors will probably call the police. But if it goes off every time a bird lands on the windowsill, the neighbors will either ignore it or ask the police to arrest *you*.

Studies show, says marriage counselor Norman Epstein, that very angry responses like breaking dishes or putting his tie in the food processor usually only escalate the problem. Either he responds in kind (there go the rest of the dishes) or he withdraws even further. If he withdraws, you may find it even more difficult to get his attention. What do you do if he ignores breaking dishes? Wreck the dishwasher?

Another time-honored strategy is the threat. If you don't do what I want, I'll leave. I'll call your mother. I'll call *my* mother. Whatever. A threat is only as good as your intention to back it up. If you really feel that leaving is your only alternative, it's only fair to say so. But there are some very sad people who felt forced to follow through on something they hadn't really thought through at all. I know a man who told his wife that if she insisted on a career, he would leave her. She went to work, he went to court, and *he's* the one who is miserable.

There are some more positive choices—not just to attract another's attention but also to keep it long enough to make real contact. No results guaranteed, you understand. No money back if dissatisfied. It's just that I find some systems are more effective than others.

For example, I know a woman who claimed her fiancé was always so busy, so absorbed in what he was doing, that she couldn't even break in long enough to let him know she needed more of his time. She cried a good bit about this but then hit on a marvelously simple solution. She wrote him a letter. *Everybody* reads his mail.

Certainly one of the most obvious ways to get a guy to pay attention to something you very much want to do is equally simple. You just do it. In some situations, this is the *only* way.

One time, in my newspaper career, I found myself working for a male editor who firmly believed that a female could write stories only about other females, and only frivolous stories, at that. I had a lot of other subjects I wanted to write about, even though, as it happens, I rather like female and/or frivolous stories, too. So I tried to get the editor to give me a serious assignment, with no success.

My answer was simply to give assignments to myself. Whenever I had free time, I got on the telephone and dug up something interesting on my own. I'd turn it in and—what else could he do?—he'd use it.

I don't claim this will work equally well everywhere or with everybody, but it is certainly a plan to ponder.

My friend Jennifer tells a story about her mother, who decided to take a job cleaning office buildings between the hours of five and seven. "You have to understand," Jennifer says, "just how startling that was to my father. He had been brought up in Ireland in the kind of household where the women don't sit down at the table until the men have finished eating. Not only had my mother decided she wanted to go out to work, which he didn't understand at all, but she had left him to handle dinner for five kids. She knew he would never have agreed to *discuss* such an awful prospect. So she just did it.

"For a while it was chaos. He thought my mother was accusing him of not supporting his family. She assured him that was not the case. But there was no way he could just ignore the situation—not with five children greeting him every night with 'What's for dinner, Daddy?'"

Jennifer recalls the outcome fondly: "He learned how to cook."

GETTING HIS ATTENTION

Psychologist Carol Tavris tells the story of a couple who fought all the time about being on time. He never was, and it drove her crazy. If they were invited out, they always arrived late. If they had tickets to a play, they missed part of the first act. Complaining got her nowhere. So what she did was go alone and meet him there. If they had two tickets, she took one. If they had to catch a plane, she left for the airport first.

If this fellow had any doubt that his wife was serious about not wanting to be late, he certainly learned otherwise. Which does not necessarily mean that he changed his ways. In fact, he didn't. It now costs double cab fare for this couple to go anywhere, and they never arrive together, but at least they don't fight about it anymore.

"Doing something" sometimes translates into *not* reacting in the usual way. For instance, you no longer sign papers unless you know what's in them. Or you no longer pick shirts off the floor if you feel very strongly that the opening in the laundry hamper is large enough for anyone to see.

My friend Ann says her father hates to spend money, even though he has plenty. Every month when the bills come in he yells about them. "For years, my mother's reaction to this was to scrimp and save and buy only absolute essentials—usually only things for the kids. When I got older I decided this was crazy. I told my mother, 'If he's going to yell anyway, you might just as well buy what you want. If you're going to put up with screaming, make it worthwhile.' It's worked out fine. He hasn't stopped yelling, but he doesn't yell *more*."

Marriage counselor Pat Wisch explains it this way:

"When I go fishing, I throw my line in the water and if the fish bite, I keep throwing my line in the same place. If they don't bite, I try somewhere else. Human beings work the same way. If someone hooks you every time he puts a line in the water, he isn't going to fish any other way." You don't have to be mean, selfish, or nasty, says Wisch, but you also don't have to be a martyr.

All of the above sounds as if you need explosives to get a guy to listen, but that's not usually so. Sometimes getting his attention is not so much a question of "whether" as of "when." Possibly you have heard it said that in real estate there are only three things to know: location, location, and location. Well, in the business we are discussing here there are also three things to know: timing, timing, and timing.

Marriage counselors have told me they advise women to make dates with guys they have been married to for twenty years. It sounds silly, but it's really just a way to convey that you need some undivided attention and also a way to arrange a time for a serious talk that suits him as well as you.

I tend not to be so formal about this kind of thing. I suppose that's because Bernie is a pretty willing listener. But I am not totally unaware of the value of timing. It seems to me that if you plan to bring up something you suspect the other does not want to hear, it is probably best to do so at some time *other than* (1) while his favorite TV show is on (unless what you have to tell him is that the house is on fire), or (2) just after he has told you he's had a veritable Murphy's Law (If anything can go wrong, it will) kind of day.

Carole Saline, coauthor of a book called *Straight Talk,*

says that just as important as *when* you say something is whether you ever say anything else. She claims that some women try to get a guy's attention only when they want to complain. It's no wonder he doesn't listen, she says, if he thinks the only messages he's going to hear are that the cat threw up, the furnace broke down, and she's having an affair.

"And how enthusiastic would *you* be to agree to sit down for a heart-to-heart talk," she asks, "if every time you did, you not only heard a new gripe, but got a recap of every wrong you'd committed in the last five years?"

Not very, to be sure. You may recall how the ancients treated the messenger who brought bad news. They blamed him for it and bopped him good. Scholars have been searching ever since—without much success—for a way to tell people things they don't want to hear.

Certainly one has to be persistent in righting a wrong; on the other hand, it's wrong to want to be right about everything at once.

I suspect that the reason Bernie and I are so ready to listen to each other's gripes, groans, and grumbles is that these things form only a minor part of our usual conversation. What Carol Saline refers to as "our praise-blame ratio" is not out of whack. A healthy amount of praise makes a percentage of blame acceptable.

And it's true we rarely dredge up ancient history, usually because we have forgotten it. You know, there's a lot to be said for a short attention span.

Another thing we do, once we have each other's attention, is actually try to hear what's being said. You might think that all we have to do is register the words, since we both speak English, but I haven't found that to be true. I often hear something other than what Bernie thinks he's saying. And vice versa.

There are times when I am so busy framing my clever reply that I actually miss the statement I'm supposed to be replying to. Or Bernie will repeat back to me what he thinks I'm telling him, and I'll say, "No, no, no, I don't mean that at all; I mean this."

But I think the main reason we get each other's attention whenever we need it with a minimum of effort is that, even if something ghastly has happened, we don't attempt to fix blame. We tend to raise issues in what might be called a neutral manner. For example, "I think we have a problem with the plumbing" is neutral; "I think you wrecked the pump again, you nitwit" is not. "I'm upset about something" is a simple statement of fact. "You are a lunatic, that's what you are" is a declaration of war.

Many of my friends mentioned this same kind of approach. "I felt our marriage needed some professional counseling if Ned and I were to avoid splitting up," Linda confided. "And I almost said, 'You need help,' but I stopped myself in time. Instead I said, 'Maybe *we* could benefit from it.' And he said, 'If you'll go, I will.' And we did."

Said Ellen, "I've found that if I say to Ray, 'I'm overwhelmed; I can't face doing the dishes,' he will nobly offer to help. But if I say, 'It's your turn to do the dishes; it's about time you did your share here,' he gets very defensive. And the dishes may end up being thrown instead of washed."

"We were talking about having a baby," said Mary, "and I explained that I was hesitant because I was afraid that I would be left to do all the work myself, that I would make all the career sacrifices. Actually, what I *wanted* to say was that I was sure he'd stick me with the work because every time he invites his mother to visit he sticks me with entertaining her. But I restrained myself. And because he wants this baby so much, we were able to talk about my fears, and he promised to share the responsibilities."

Aggie chipped in: "When Phil comes after me and starts yelling that this or that is my fault and that I can't do anything right, I stay cool and just refuse to discuss the issue. I tell him that when he is calm enough to talk about what's wrong and not just call me names, I'll be happy to talk to him. In his more rational moments, he admits we never got much settled when we both did nothing but scream."

All the experts say that it is best to keep your head when you feel like chopping someone else's off. It is best to stay calm. I am not always able to manage that, I have to admit, but that doesn't mean I don't think it's wonderful advice.

This brings to mind an interview with Paul Newman that appeared in *Time* magazine. It seems that Newman's actress wife Joanne Woodward had handed him a movie script and suggested it would be fun if they did it together. Relates Newman, "I read it and said, 'Joanne, it's just a bunch of one-liners.' And she said, 'You son of a bitch, I've been carting your children around, taking care of them at the expense of my career, taking care of you and your house.' And I said, 'That is what I said. It's a terrific script. I can't think of anything I'd rather do.'"

Proving that even to the most sensible rules there are always exceptions.

8

THE GARY COOPER SYNDROME

I'm convinced that if women could redesign men the first thing they would change is the way men talk.

You know what men say about women—that they talk too much. But women complain that most men don't talk *enough*, or not about the right things, anyway. We seem to be a nation of Gary Coopers: "Yup.... Nope.... Have you met my horse?"

There has been a lot of research into this. Probably the most famous is that of anthropologist Ray Birdwhistel, who equipped one hundred couples with microphones to determine how much conversation goes on between them during the course of a week. He eliminated all grunts, all simple announcements like "Dinner is on the table" and such minimal replies as "Yes, dear" and came up with a grand total of twenty-eight minutes a week! Imagine. All it takes is two good fights and a whole month's allotment is shot.

The complaints I have heard are not about silence per se, but rather about silence on certain subjects. Silence about emotions, feelings, love, passion, a lack of words expressing appreciation, a dearth of information about his life away from home, a paucity of good gossip.

In a way, a song sung by Willie Nelson, "Always on My Mind," makes this point. It is all about how men don't say what they feel. Supposedly it is the lament of a man whose woman has walked out on him. He admits he didn't treat her "quite as good as I should have." The guy goes on to moan that she shouldn't have left him. She should have understood that even if he seemed cold and indifferent, in fact, she was always on his mind.

Well, women are saying, it's about time that what is on his mind and in his heart occasionally reaches his lips.

It doesn't even have to be mushy. All Humphrey Bogart says to Ingrid Bergman in *Casablanca* is "We'll always have Paris" and "Here's looking at you, kid," and yet, women have been swooning for forty years.

My friend Marie says her Hank is a perfect example of the kind of guy Nelson is singing about. Hank is a basically nice man who tells his *secretary* how wonderful his family is. "I stopped by his office," said Marie, "and his secretary knew our older daughter Terry had made the sweater he was wearing and that he loved it. The secretary knew I'd made a very special dinner the other night and he had loved that, too. So I said to him, 'Why didn't you tell Terry you liked the sweater?' He said, 'She knows.' I said, 'Why didn't you tell me the dinner was terrific?' He got all flustered and said, 'I ate it, didn't I?'"

A few years ago, according to the *Journal of Marriage and the Family*, three midwestern professors decided to study typical family "communication styles." They asked men and women to comment separately on how they would behave in certain situations.

One of their scenarios presumed that the man has some problem at work that he is very worried about. Would he:

1. Say nothing, but be crabby around the house?
2. Act as if nothing is bothering him?
3. Not admit that he is worried personally, but try to get his wife's reaction by bringing the problem up as if it were happening to someone else?
4. Say he is worried, let his wife know about it, and talk it over?

The overwhelming majority of wives recognized their spouses as example 1, the man who reveals nothing but acts like King Kong. What they wanted, they said, was that fellow from example 4, the one who confides in his partner and allows her to be involved. The husbands, it must be admitted, tended to see themselves in example 2, a horde of stalwart stoics. What's more, they thought this was the proper way for both men *and women* to behave. How discouraging.

No doubt about it, "communication style" is an area in which men and women are incredibly different. And, interestingly, this difference seems to start all the way back in the crib.

Female babies are more verbal than male babies. Is this because mothers talk more to little girl babies? Science cannot say. The fact is that by age four, most little girls will be talking words while most little boys still prefer to make noises (*Brrrrrr; bang!*). Eventually, of course, both sexes acquire an equal ability to handle the language but not, apparently, an equal interest in the full range of subjects that language can be applied to.

I hope we all agree that the differences between men and women do not mean that a woman can't work as a plumber or that a man shouldn't work as a telephone operator. I hope we have all given up the notion that men and women *have to be* different in rigid and clearly specified ways. But differences certainly do exist.

Let's face it, it's still true that, by and large, women are more interested than men in fashion, that women are more interested than men in maintaining social contacts. (Did you know that women buy 90 percent of all greeting cards sold in the United States?) He is more likely to be found at a ball game, she at a flower show. When lost, she is more likely to ask directions; he'll want to study the map. He tends to heat up faster in bed. And this business of how we talk is the biggest difference of all. When it comes to a willingness to reveal inner feelings, she tends to be bubbling champagne, he tends to be a cork, and the result is nothing to celebrate.

Just how different men are in this area was brought home to me one time when a civic organization asked me to participate in a "roast" for a well-known local personality. The program chairman explained that they had never before asked a woman to participate in this annual event, but they thought it was about time. Naturally, I accepted, but I was sorry later.

What I discovered is that a roast, by definition, is a male-only event. Only men would think of honoring somebody by having a series of speakers insult him. Now, I am rarely at a loss for words (I definitely qualify as a talkative woman), but I really had to struggle to come up with something to say. Think about it: how many women would show their pleasure at bumping into an old friend by saying, "What have you been up to, you old son of a bitch?"

When Shere Hite compiled the *Hite Report on Male*

Sexuality, she was dismayed to find that the questionnaires filled out by men weren't half so interesting as those filled out by women for the previous report on female sexuality. The women went into depth about how they felt about their sex lives, but the men (with some exceptions, including one who even sent a drawing along to illustrate his interests) tried to say as little as possible. One wonders why they bothered to reply at all.

Speech pathologist Lillian Glass claims that the difference between male and female speech patterns causes many a marital dispute. For example, she says, women tend to use flowery adjectives like "marvelous," "stunning," and "exquisite" whereas men prefer to stick to low-key descriptions. And so when she says, "How do you like my dress?" and he says, "It's nice," she may say, "If you don't like it say so." Whereupon he may say, "I said it was nice. What do you want me to do? Turn handsprings?"

The battle, Dr. Glass says, can be fueled by the fact that many men make requests that sound like commands— as in "Get me a beer." Even if she is standing next to the refrigerator, she may be annoyed enough to reply, "Get it yourself." He then says, "What's the matter with you? Is one lousy beer too much to ask?"

You may wonder why this women doesn't just say "I will, if you say please" or why this man wouldn't think of saying please in the first place. Dr. Glass wonders, too. She thinks that women should not be so quick to take offense and that men would do well to adjust their speech patterns.

Of course, sometimes a request sounds like a command because it *is* a command. On the TV show "Couples," psychiatrist Walter Brackelmanns tried to get a bossy husband to understand that his habit of ordering his wife around was making her angry.

"But I don't order her around," the husband protested. "I only make requests."

"Do you get angry if she says no to your requests?" Brackelmanns asked him.

"Of course," said the husband, "because that's her job."

Brackelmanns explained that making a request she can't refuse is *not* asking; it's telling. Clearly, vocabulary isn't everything.

In any case, it isn't that men do not know that women respond best when spoken to with diplomacy and charm. Everybody knows that's why Casanova made out so well. Unfortunately, however, these attributes do not necessarily come with men as standard equipment.

There's an old joke about this. A young man complains that he isn't making a hit with the opposite sex. A friend asks him if he pays his dates compliments. The young man admits that he doesn't. "Well, you try that," says his friend. "Women just love compliments." Later the friend sees the young man and asks if the suggestion worked. The young man regretfully shakes his head.

"You paid your date a compliment?" asks his friend.

"Yeah."

"What did you say?"

"I said, 'For a fat girl, you don't eat much.'"

Robert "Big Murf" Murphy, of the rock group Neighbor's Complaint, claims he used to earn good money when he was in the navy by writing love letters for his shipmates. He would write stuff like this: "The expression on your face in your picture makes my pillow softer." And the guys loved it because the girls loved it. Of course, allows Murphy, sometimes a girl would write back, "This letter is not you. You never could talk. You probably can't talk now. Who wrote this letter? Tell him I love *him*. Ha ha."

To say we long for a man to talk to us, to tell us what he feels, is not to discount the value of that look in his eye, those actions that speak louder than words, the quiet hug that is so full of meaning, the silence that is more companionable than any ten conversations could be. Not at all.

It is just that when a guy tends to be silent most of the time, when he confides rarely or not at all, when he speaks only in directives, when he can't bring himself to say "You are a wonderful cook" (much less, as in *Cyrano de Bergerac*, "Your name is like a golden bell hung in my heart, and when I think of you, I tremble, and the bell swings and rings...") well, then, women begin to feel unwanted, unloved, unappreciated, and bored.

Frankly, it doesn't make a lot of difference whether this is a matter of nature or nurture, whether it is a deliberate conspiracy or a dumb mistake, whether it is a recent innovation or a problem that dates back to the days when all men did was hunt and grunt while women hung around in the cave discussing wall paintings. Something should be done about it.

For if a woman feels ignored, she may pick a fight just to get some kind of communication going. If a man is unable to confide his feelings, he may feel lonely and alone and not know what to do about it.

What good does it do for marriage counselors to claim that a lot of problems can be solved if two people will just talk them out, if the two people involved never talk?

Psychiatrist Brackelmanns says he sometimes has to

get a couple to agree just to *look* at each other. Then he introduces them. "Maryann, this is Harry. Harry, this is Maryann. You've been together for five years now, and it's time you got to know each other."

What to do. Well, it is very doubtful that you can turn most guys into poets. I suspect that if you have a Gary Cooper, you aren't going to turn him into a Phil Donahue, and that's that. Even so, you may still be able to increase the quantity and maybe even the quality of conversation. You may be able to make it easier rather than harder for him to open up and confide in you.

First, let's discuss this business of increasing the conversation. Talking about this with my friends certainly increased *our* conversations. *Everybody* had something to say.

Probably because so many of my friends are in the news business—either in newspapers or TV—their opinions leaned heavily toward the techniques talk show hosts and reporters use when they want somebody they are interviewing to talk. For example, you ask questions that cannot be answered yes or no. I have been a TV talk show host, and I am here to tell you that there is nothing more terrible than realizing your show is on the air live and your guest has just swallowed his tongue. I have found that even the glibbest, most articulate types can freeze up when it suddenly strikes them that they are on the air. You can tell this from the funny noises they make: "Uh, uh, oh, ooo, ah..."

If you ask them questions that can be answered yes or no, that is all they will say. "Do you think the workers should go on strike?" "Yes." So you have to ask, "Why do you think the workers should go on strike?" That will force a guest to put a whole sentence together. This works just as well at home. My friend Julie tells me that when John comes home, she doesn't say, "Did anyone get fired today?" She asks, "Who got fired today and what did they do?"

Another tried and true interview technique is to tell your story first and ask the other side to respond. Most of us hate to feel we are being put on the spot, so if the reporter reveals his or her feelings or doubts about a touchy matter even before asking a question, that often enables the other side simply to relax and either agree or disagree.

Sometimes, of course, the way to start a lively conversation is simply to find a subject that both sides are interested in. Some of the marriage counselors I talked to told me that a woman will claim that her husband never talks to her, while the husband claims that he has tried to talk to her about his business but that she only rolls her eyes as if to say, "Not that again." The husband will claim that it's the wife who doesn't talk to him. She then says that she tried that very morning to talk to him about her mother, but he developed a glazed look that said, "Not her again." Oh, dear. Maybe if he went into business with her mother?

Finally, one of my friends says that she encouraged her husband to speak up a little more just by making a fuss over him every time he did. If he merely said, "That's a nice dress," she would say, "It makes me feel so good when you say that."

Next, there is the matter of a man being open and willing to confide in you. One of my friends says that the first thing to do about this is make sure you really want it. She claims she urged her fiancé to open up, to reveal his weaknesses and fears, to let himself be vulnerable. So he did, and now she's not sure she wants to marry him. She liked his stiff upper lip, Rock of Gibraltar, totally in control image better.

She turned out to be more old style than she had thought. Obviously you can't have a new style relationship if either of the partners hides or disguises great chunks of himself or herself from the other.

To encourage openness, you must provide a "safe" environment. This is true anywhere. I know a guy who used to work for a boss who said he wanted suggestions from his employees. "Tell me anything," this boss said, "even that I'm doing something wrong, because I am very concerned about making this company profitable." This guy I know took the man at his word and mentioned something the boss was doing wrong. Next thing he knew, he was collecting unemployment. And, as far as he knows, the boss has never received a second suggestion.

Therefore, if you encourage a man to reveal his inner feelings, you cannot then make him sorry he did so. You can't tell your friends what he said; you can't use it as evidence against him in your next quarrel; you can't, in short, make him sorry he trusted you. This can be very frustrating, of course, but you want the same from him, don't you?

I think one of the greatest stimulators of mutual confidence I know is something Bernie taught me. And that is that you can reveal a problem, confess anger, or express emotion and not want or expect the listener to do a damn thing about it other than listen. Isn't that terrific?

It used to bother me if Bernie told me something that I could do nothing about. "Oh, my," I would say, "I just

THE GARY COOPER SYNDROME

don't know what to tell you to do." He assured me I didn't have to know. What he needed was simply a sounding board. Talking to me helped him think the problem through.

And I have asked the same of him: "I know you can't solve this. I don't even want you to solve this. I really want to work it out myself. But I have to talk about it." And we do. Sometimes all you want is someone to say, "You're right. That's rotten."

This isn't to say we should never make a suggestion. And sometimes the suggestion is even accepted. Other times it may be rejected. But we never get fired.

The fact that Bernie does talk things out with me is one of the things I love best about him. But I also have to say that I love his ability, at times, to stay quiet—when I have just done something dumb, for example. He knows it was dumb. I know it. And he knows that I know it. But he pretends nothing has happened. He doesn't say a word. There are times when a Gary Cooper is the most desirable male of all.

9

GOING THROUGH NAGGING WITHDRAWAL

Nagging is woman's oldest weapon. When I married I promised, in a weak moment, never to nag. I thought I'd given away my birthright, but it's one of the best things I ever did.

The worst thing about nagging is that it doesn't work—not well and not often, anyway. The next worst thing about it is that it gives a man a weapon he can use against a woman. He can accuse her of being a nag.

She asks him to take out the trash. He says yes, but he doesn't. She asks him again. He still doesn't. She insists. He postpones. She demands. Now he is indignant. He says she is nagging him. Clever him. Now *she's* the bad guy.

When I told a friend of mine that I planned to write about nagging, she said, "I hope you are going to define what that means, because in my house what I call reminding, prompting, or suggesting, he calls nagging. If I tell him that the lawn he has promised to mow has a good chance of being declared a U.S. National Wilderness Area, he says I'm nagging. If we are driving someplace and I say, 'Don't forget to make a right turn at Elm,' he will say, 'I have the same directions you have. You don't have to nag.' And yet, if I say nothing because I don't want to be accused of nagging, and we go *past* Elm, he'll say, 'Why didn't you say something?'"

Ah, yes, what *is* nagging? My dictionary calls it "persistent petty faultfinding, scolding or urging." It says the word comes from a Scandinavian expression meaning to gnaw, bite, or hurt. And although this clearly is something anyone can do to anyone else, it is generally assumed that nagging is a nasty trick played on men by women. In fact, a Pennsylvania man who killed his wife offered her nagging as his defense. He claimed he couldn't help himself; her nagging goaded him into picking up the shotgun. He appealed his case all the way to the state supreme court, which ruled against him, regretfully it seemed, on the grounds that "if nagging were justification for homicide, few married men would ever be convicted."

Somehow men have managed to escape the onus of being called nags; unfairly so, I think. Even if they don't do it as much, surely they cause women to do it far more. After all, if a woman does make the same request over and over again, doesn't she do so only because her original request has never been answered?

It seems to me we have never given proper recognition to the fact that nagging is often more frustrating to the nagger than to the naggee. One of the angriest people I've ever met was a woman who'd spent some twenty years nagging a man who was determined to ignore her. I attended her murder trial. She finally ran over him six times with their car. Twice would have done the job adequately, but, as he would have said himself if he could have, she had a tendency to repeat herself.

The difference between a nag and reminder, I think, is only a matter of perception. Alerting the absentminded professor that he is once again pouring cream into the goldfish bowl and fish food into his coffee is generally taken as a friendly warning. Whereas alerting the absentminded husband that he is once again reading the newspaper instead of taking out the garbage is generally viewed as criticism or complaint, which, of course, it is.

And yet in both cases we are really saying the same thing: "You are goofing up." The professor cheerfully acknowledges it; the husband does not. Obviously, from a male point of view, nagging is being reminded whenever you don't want to be reminded. And from a female point of view it is having to say something fifty times that should have to be mentioned only once, or not at all.

Nagging is decidedly old style because it implies that a woman believes she is doing what is expected of her but her man isn't doing what is expected of him and also because it implies that while *he* has the power to command, *she* can only annoy. New style women do not want to nag, but sometimes feel they are trapped into doing it when dealing with an old style man.

The question is: just how old style do you have to be to get your man to do what you want done? At the very least, it would seem to me that a new style woman can avoid the three major categories of nagging that have landed women in the most trouble throughout history. These are the techniques that have proven almost totally ineffective at anything other than making everybody angry.

The first is the earlybird reminder. A woman is guilty of this when she begins to nag somebody for not doing something before he has had a decent chance not to do it. The problem here is a basic lack of trust. The woman is so sure that her man will let her down, probably because he has let her down twelve or two hundred times before, that she begins to remind him that he has promised to do something long before he can fairly be accused of having failed to do it. He resents the implication that he is falling down on the job, even if he is, and thus becomes even more determined to do nothing.

Let us say that George has promised to fix the door before winter sets in. It is now July. And we hear his wife say, "Don't forget you promised to fix the door. How come you aren't fixing the door? When are you going to fix the door? Aren't you going to fix the door? Why are you going out the door? *George, come back here!*"

An even more futile form of nagging is exemplified by the chronic asker of a question to which she already knows the answer but doesn't like it: "Why aren't you as rich as my brother Harry?" or "Why don't you just tell that boss of yours off?"

This is a much less sympathetic type of nagger; although she also feels let down, what she is asking for may be something beyond the power of the man to give.

This is *very* old style, of course, because usually this kind of nagger has no outlet for her ambition—and expects none—other than her husband and/or children. Therefore if her man has not succeeded as she had hoped, if she has not reached the status in life she expected, then she gets him. And gets him. And gets him.

You might think that this sort of behavior would have converted hosts of old style men to new style thinking decades ago. You might think he would have enjoyed being able to say, "Now that you bring it up, why aren't *you* as rich as your brother Harry?" At least this might lead to an interesting discussion of the equal pay act. But no, the more typical male response is a snarl, "Get off my back," which leads nowhere at all.

The most creative futile form of nagging is that in which the woman picks on the man for something that has nothing to do with what is really upsetting her.

Let's say a woman feels the man is taking her for granted. She feels she is doing more than her share and he doesn't even appreciate it. She doesn't say this, but she broods about it and then makes a huge fuss about whether he has remembered to bring home a loaf of bread or whether he has dropped an ash on the rug.

This kind of nagging is very often expressed in action as opposed to words. The story of Fran the towel snatcher is a perfect case in point. I learned about Fran by watching "Couples," the syndicated television series in which real people tell their problems to psychiatrist Walter Brackelmanns. On this particular program, Fran's husband Rex complains about Fran's habit of waiting until he is in the shower before gathering up the towels for the laundry. It seems that Fran does not immediately replace the used towels with fresh ones, which means that Rex frequently finds himself naked, wet, and totally towelless.

Rex said he'd told Fran many times just to let his towel be, but she wouldn't. "Well, I can't just let them grow," said Fran.

Brackelmanns immediately recognized that there was more to this fight than dry terry cloth. Sure enough, it turned out that Rex, by his own admission, was a domestic tyrant—old style to his very core. "What would it take to make everything okay between you and Fran?" asked Brackelmanns. "She should do everything I say," replied Rex. Aha.

Fran bitterly resented being ordered about, but although she was angry she was also afraid. So instead of confronting Rex directly and telling him this in plain terms, she resorted to guerrilla warfare. She would "forget" to replace his towel. She would "mistakenly" undercook his eggs. She was always half a beat off and half a step behind.

Put another way, she was getting him. And getting him. And getting him. She was "persistently scolding" him, but she wasn't doing it with words. She was attacking him for something small because she was being denied something big. Fran was tormenting Rex because he was tormenting her. And if that isn't a classic case of nagging, what is?

I phoned Brackelmanns to find out what finally happened to Rex and Fran, and he told me he'd heard that Rex solved his problem—but not Fran's—by building a new bathroom with a towel closet he can reach from the shower. So he's still in control, and one has to wonder what Fran will do next to assert herself. Maybe she'll decide to *clean* the towel closet at the crucial moment. "I think I saw some mold." Possibly she will turn to some nontowel technique such as turning off his hot water. "There must be something wrong with the heater, dear." One thing is sure. She'll get him.

My own brief foray into nagging was a variation on theme number one. When we first married, Bernie was in the process of earning a doctorate. He had completed all the course work without my help and in fact without even knowing of my existence, and he was now engaged in the final step—writing a dissertation. There was a deadline for completing it, which seemed to me to be impossibly close. I worried that he would not get it done.

"Aren't you going to work on the dissertation?" I asked him at any hour when his attention seemed to be diverted elsewhere. "When are you going to work on the dissertation? How can you be reading the paper when the dissertation isn't finished?... Go for a walk? Are you nuts? What about the dissertation?"

"Nag. Nag. Nag," said Bernie.

Who me? The very model of enlightened womanhood?

None other.

Of course, I only wanted to be helpful but, as Bernie pointed out, what I was saying was that I didn't trust him to finish it. I was giving him the distinct impression that I thought he wasn't grown up enough to handle his own affairs.

Oh, dear. That put me in a very difficult position. I couldn't even argue that he had let me down before, because he hadn't. I didn't even *know* him before. So I promised to stop nagging about the dissertation—and never to *start* nagging ever about anything else. As I say, I got carried away.

After that, if he read the newspaper, I said nothing. If he wanted to go for a walk, I went for a walk, too. And he finished the dissertation anyway. He stayed up until 4:00 A.M. when the mood was on him, fueled by black coffee he made himself because helpful old me was fast asleep.

You may be thinking, But what if he hadn't finished it? Would I feel so smug about my promise? In this era of joint property laws, is it not to a woman's interest that a man get ahead in his employment? If getting that degree would mean a job advancement or higher salary for him, was it right to leave this vital matter totally in his hands?

If he had not come through, might I not have turned into a category two nagger (She: "If you'd finished your dissertation, we wouldn't be living like this") or even category three (He: "You ripped up my newspaper again? Why do you do that?")?

Obviously, it is easy to give up nagging if you get what you want. The opposite also is true. But the fact remains that I gave up nagging *before* I knew the outcome, and I can tell you that I have also chosen not to nag even when I suspect he's not going to do something, and it turns out I am absolutely right. Which is not to say, I will never (heh heh) remind, or prompt, or suggest.

I'll explain. What I have done is to exclude from my repertoire those aspects of reminding, prompting, and suggesting that never do any good anyway. Take the matter of the dissertation.

First, I was clearly blaming him for not doing something he hadn't yet not done. I think he was right to feel insulted. Since insults have a long history of being counterproductive, not nagging in such situations is probably to your advantage.

Second, I really was in a no-win situation anyway. Bernie knew best when he felt motivated to write, and that certainly wasn't after having a fight with me. I found that

GOING THROUGH NAGGING WITHDRAWAL

even when my nagging succeeded, I wasn't getting results. That's definitely a time to stop.

Third, I was quibbling over how he did something that was strictly his to do. This is rarely effective. I don't like it if Bernie tells me how to do things I consider my business, and I credit him with feeling the same way.

I explained this to my daughter one day when she called me in tears to report she'd had a fight with her boyfriend. He, it seems, was building a patio the Wrong Way.

"I have told him and told him until I'm blue in the face," said Carole, "that he is piling the bricks for the patio right where the shrubbery is going to be planted. If the shrubs are delivered before the patio is finished, he's only going to have to move all those bricks. It *doesn't make sense* when he could so easily pile them out of the way in the first place."

Little did she know she had called Naggers Anonymous. I was more than eager to pass my theories along. "Let me ask you this," I said. "If the bricks have to be moved, who will move them? Will you have to do it?"

"No, he'll move them," she said, "but that's the point. He'll have to do double work. And that's wasteful. It's dumb."

"That's what you think," I said. "But maybe he enjoys moving bricks. Maybe he would rather lift bricks than lift weights. Of course, it's annoying to watch something being done in a method you don't approve of, but the easiest thing to do is don't watch. If the bricks are not going to fall on you, if they are not in *your* way, and if, finally, *you* are not the one who will have to solve the problem, let him worry about them. That way you save your reminding, prompting, and suggesting energies for something that affects you in a more direct way."

In my opinion, the kid was in danger of reverting to old style thinking, and I had to save her. I had to convince her that this wasn't only a question of whether her pal resented her advice. What really worried me was that she seemed to feel responsible for making sure that he did whatever he was doing the Right Way.

Women, of course, have long been told this is so. How many times, for example, have you seen articles with titles that say something like this: "Wives, Are You Killing Your Husband?" Invariably these articles advise women to be sure their man does things the Right Way. He should eat a proper diet, he should go to the doctor, he should exercise often, he should brush his teeth three times a day. Presumably, if he doesn't do these things, *she* has failed. *She* is killing him.

My attitude about such advice is: tell *him*, don't tell me. I am killing him only if I slip arsenic into his cereal. Otherwise, *he* is doing it. I may not like it, but I am not responsible for it. I suggest. I even clip articles that apply to *him* as fair warning. But after that, he's on his own. I thought Carole was right to bring up the shrubbery issue, since her friend may have been unaware that he was making double work for himself. But nagging him about it was quite another matter. It was not the most effective use of *her* time.

In fact, the more I think about it, the more convinced I become that nagging, although it is thought of as a woman's weapon, was probably invented by a male secret agent who infiltrated our lines.

GOING THROUGH NAGGING WITHDRAWAL

After all, men have such terrific defenses against even perfectly reasonable nagging—the kind concerned with things they say they will do and then don't. They ignore. They shrug off. They say yes-yes while they turn off the hearing aid. They dismiss her demands as trivial. They can't take out the garbage when they are occupied with assessing our foreign policy.

Sometimes, just to "shut her up," a man will do what the woman wishes. She gets her way, but the neighbors feel sorry for *him*. Hmph! My friend Nan says that when she has kept after Pete for weeks to finish some simple chore, she will finally lose her temper and just *shriek* or *break plates* or *slam the door*. And then Pete will say she's being irrational, just like a woman, although when she's being "rational" he finds her easy to ignore.

Some weapon that is. It's like having a shotgun that on a rare occasion may actually hit a target but usually wounds its owner in the foot.

There has to be another way—other than doing everything ourselves, because that's not fair. And other than suffering in silence, because that's impossible.

When I asked my friends as well as professional counselors how to deal with nagging (prompting-and-reminding division), everybody was very quick to say, "Don't." But on the question of how to get results without nagging, they tended to sigh and roll their eyes and say they are still tinkering with their formulas.

Everybody seemed to agree that if you are dealing with an old style man who wants what he wants when he wants it and wants to do what he wants to do when he wants to do it, no perfect solution is in sight. But that is not to say they had no suggestions to make. That is not to say the situation can't be made better.

We all agreed that the first step in going through nagging withdrawal is to sharply limit those issues about which you are willing to remind, prompt, and suggest.

The woman who is seen as a nagger is the one who is "always on his back." By more carefully picking one's targets, this image is eliminated. My own experience was that this not only put Bernie in a more receptive frame of mind, it did that for me, too. So, as I said before, I skip those things that he can't do anyway, those that I can't yet prove he isn't going to do, and those that are his to do, because they are only indirectly related to me. That eliminates an enormous amount, yet still leaves plenty to work on.

The next step is to do all reminding, prompting, and urging that is still required in the most effective way.

That definitely means stating what you think is important, including trivial tasks, in a very direct way, even though some people claim this is unfeminine.

Writer Bob Schwabach claims that the reason men don't nag is that when a man feels wronged, he mentally hauls off and socks somebody. It isn't an actual attack, it's an attitude. His theory is that because a woman can't even imagine herself slugging anybody, she resorts to nagging and manipulation. "Women," says Schwabach, "are masters, um, make that mistresses, of indirection."

The problem of being indirect, of course, is that, as in the case of Rex and Fran, it is like sending a ransom note in Sanskrit. Even if the recipient somehow senses his beloved is in trouble, how will he know where to send the money?

When my friends Bill and Caroline were dating, Bill frequently called Caroline at her office. She worked with four women and one man. If Caroline wasn't around, the women always gave her Bill's message, but the man never bothered to. The women decided to teach him a lesson by not taking his messages or by fouling them up or by making them up. When Caroline gleefully told Bill about this, he was scornful: "You think you're teaching him a lesson, but he probably can't figure out what's going on." The next time Bill called he said to this fellow, "I don't understand why you don't give Caroline my messages. Don't you know how to read and write?" That time the guy got the message, and so did Caroline.

Another ineffective method of nagging is the overstated generalization. This occurs when she has asked him to fix the broken door hinge and he doesn't and she says, "You always forget. You never do what I want."

Probably she means that he has forgotten the door hinge before or that he forgets things quite often. However, it is rare to find someone who always or never does anything. Therefore, once she uses those words, he is not only on the defensive, he is also on the attack. He can argue about "never" and "always" until she becomes as unhinged as the door.

The more specific you can be, the better. The more specific he is, the better off you are. If he promises to fix a door someday, the promise unfulfilled is not exactly broken.

If he promises to fix it by Wednesday and does not, you are surely free to remind him.

Sometimes the best form of reminder is to say nothing at all, but just wait. Psychologist Ann Spector commented that just as any two-year-old knows that if he whines long enough his mother will probably break down and give him a cookie, sometimes a man will deliberately ignore a task he is supposed to do because he knows his wife will eventually give up and do it herself. Only the woman involved knows whether it is worth it to her to hold out longer or to cave in. Since nagging won't do it, she might as well save her breath.

One time I attended a course given for corporate managers on how to motivate their employees to get the job done. Not being a corporate manager, I was there only to write about it. Anyway, in this course, we were shown a film in which a newly appointed supervisor, eager to make good, comes into his office and—horrors!—spots his first assistant casually reading the newspaper. "You are supposed to be finishing the Glutch account, not reading the paper!" the boss cries. Instead of cringing in fear, however, the assistant gets angry and threatens to "take this up with the head of the department."

We were then told that this supervisor had made a terrible error. What he had done was not efficient. A good manager would simply have asked the employee if he could count on the Glutch report by four o'clock that day. If the employee wants to read the paper but skip lunch to get the report done, who cares as long as it's done? If he doesn't do it, then the supervisor has something to complain about.

GOING THROUGH NAGGING WITHDRAWAL

I didn't know they taught corporate managers to avoid nagging. It turns out they do. They just call it something else, since managers are still predominantly male. We were told that good managers get better results from inspiring, convincing, encouraging, and praising than from accusing, attacking, and threatening. I'm sure there is a moral in that for all of us.

It is as important to recognize when your beloved has lived up to what is expected of him as it is to remind him when he hasn't. And this is something you might let him know that he can do for you.

One final word on the subject of going through nagging withdrawal: you don't have to accept that something is nagging just because he says it is. If Jack promises to climb the beanstalk and doesn't, his love has every right to ask him to get on the stick. If you offer a word of caution just as the love of your life is about to walk off a cliff, he may insist he can fly, but you are not nagging.

Men accuse women of nagging when, in fact, the women are merely reminding them of a deal they made and didn't live up to. A very unmanly, unsportsmanlike thing to do. Some men accuse women of nagging when they merely make a helpful suggestion *once*. They do this to make us feel guilty, so that while they have us on the defensive, they can be lying in the hammock, not taking out the trash.

If you swear off unessential nagging and stick to plain old reminding and suggesting, you have nothing to feel guilty about. And if he then does those things that are really most important, he'll have nothing to feel guilty about.

The fact that I don't nag Bernie does not mean he now does everything he promises to do. He knows perfectly well that I renege on some of my promises, too. I have lists of them. What we do, I think, is focus on the imperative. If I run out of milk just before company is coming, he'll rescue me right away. But on the matter of sorting through and getting rid of those boxes of papers in the spare room, which he said he would do last weekend, I figure maybe in five years if I'm lucky—and ten years is just as likely, too. I can live with that. And that's just as well. I'm sure I'll have to.

10

TWO CAN SWEEP AS NEATLY AS ONE

My neighbor Lindsay says that when she and her great love are out in public, he out-machos John Wayne. He'll make remarks about "women's work" and "woman's place" and all of that, but she doesn't care because she knows that at home, behind the drawn window shades, he's the one who does the dishes.

For her, that's what counts. Lindsay says there is no way we can claim a new era has swept in for women until men start reaching for brooms. And, judging from the number of complaints I've heard on this subject, that's a very popular idea.

What I call the "doesn't-he-live-here-too? syndrome" makes a lot of women very angry indeed. I doubt that it ranks with such biggies as money (who spends it and for what), time (how much he spends with her), or children (how to raise them) in conflict-causing potential, but it's gaining.

A 1965–66 national survey by psychologist John Pleck showed that only 19 percent of wives wanted their husbands to help with household chores. In 1973 a similar study showed the number had risen to 23 percent. Only two years later, it had jumped to 29 percent. Pleck noted that the women who wanted help from husbands included both job-holding wives and full-time homemakers. The former were more interested in help with housework, the latter more interested in help with children. That number can only have grown.

For some women, this will never be an issue because they *like* housework. I know some who find it relaxing to come home and iron after working in an office all day. There are times I feel that way about cleaning out the silverware drawer. It's a welcome change of pace. Still, I think most new style women would scorn the notion that it is exclusively a female responsibility to care for children and to keep both house and housemate clean and neat. I frequently hear such unanswerable questions as "Why do I have to ask him to empty the ashtray? Can't he see it's full?" and "Why can he never take the garbage out unless I remind him?" and "How can he pass the clothes dryer fourteen times and never think to remove the dry clothes, half of which are *his*?"

The garbage lament, of course, has been around for a while—"Harry, when are you going to get these dinosaur bones out of the cave?"—but not so the expectation that a man in the same house with a woman would empty an ashtray or a dryer.

I can't claim my survey on this subject was very scientific. It's just that whenever I talked to women about being half of a new style–old style combination, I found that almost invariably they produced a housework example to make a point. Something is definitely going on.

It seems to me that for many women, a man's attitude toward sharing the responsibilities of a home symbolizes his attitude toward her.

TWO CAN SWEEP
AS NEATLY AS ONE

An advertising woman in New York told me about a day in which she was to make a major presentation and was very nervous about it. Just before the meeting, her husband phoned her—he was home packing for a business trip—to ask where he could find a new bottle of deodorant. "I screamed at him, 'Would I call you just before an incredibly important meeting to ask you about *deodorant?*'" She says he still doesn't understand why she was upset.

I was fascinated by the number of complaints that came, not from women whose men refused to do any so-called women's work at all, but rather from those whose men had agreed to share the chores, but who weren't doing it very well.

Some of the comments went like this:

"Wouldn't you think a man who can build a whole house could figure out which button to push on a washer?"

"If a woman can learn to operate a jet plane, don't you think a man can learn to dust?"

"To me, the words 'cleaning up after dinner' mean wiping the tabletop as well as doing the dishes. I tell him the job is only half done, and he acts as if he doesn't understand what I'm saying. I can't *believe* it. The man has *two* advanced *degrees*, and he doesn't know enough to wipe the *tabletop.*"

"Dan agreed to take over the laundry in order to help out. And although he is very good at remembering to do it, what's not good is the way he does it. He has perfected a system in which everything, including permanent press, comes out wrinkled. Since Dan took over the laundry, I do more ironing than ever before."

"Harold can do open-heart surgery, but if I ask him to scrape a carrot, he leaves most of it in the garbage. At least he doesn't ask me to put the scraper in a sterilizer before he'll touch it."

"Will is wonderful about taking Sandy to nursery school whenever I suggest it. But somehow it seems never to occur to him alone. One morning I was sick and, of course, Will took over as I knew he would. But later, when I asked him something about combing Sandy's hair, he looked blank. 'You didn't say anything about hair.'"

"Yeah, he helps. But grudgingly. He always makes it clear that he is being extraordinarily kind and noble toward that half of the household whose task this *really* is."

You may well wonder why—when so many women would be happy if their men merely stopped throwing underwear on the floor, much less agree to run it through the washer—there would be this kind of complaint. What I gathered was that these women feel the men are sending them a message that reads, "This sort of thing is beneath me, but of course it is not beneath you." It is the message, more than the manner of its transmission, that is making them mad.

But it occurred to me more than once, as I listened to these positively pitiful plaints of man's inhumanity to woman, that possibly—not for sure, but possibly—many women are misreading the message.

I agree that if a man just assumes the woman will clean up after him, if night after night, she is still cooking and washing and sweeping and feeling exhausted and worn out while he has his feet up on the couch, well, she has a

TWO CAN SWEEP AS NEATLY AS ONE

right to be resentful. But how about that guy who tries and messes up?

We were talking about this at lunch one day. We had gotten into a debate about one husband who agreed to vacuum the living room rug but didn't do the corners.

"If a man cuts corners," commented Connie, "it is because he is trying to get her to say, 'Never mind, I'll do it myself.' It's a trick. It's a ploy. And they only do it because it works."

And Nan observed that in household matters men seem to be masters of the Mulligan. This is a golfing term that means you swing at the ball and then either miss or hit it into the woods and then pretend it never happened. "Ah, my turn, was it? I was just fooling around while I waited." Men claim they don't see the dirt in the corners. "Dirt? Where? Corner? What corners?"

"Everybody knows," Connie added mournfully, "that the worst part of vacuuming is not pushing the cleaner around, but taking it out of the closet, unwinding the cord, moving the furniture and putting everything back. If I have to do all or part of that later to get at the corners, what good is he?"

"Isn't it possible," I asked, "that you are getting discouraged too soon? He doesn't like to vacuum, but he's making an effort. Can't you give him ten points for trying? Even if it is more trouble for you right now, isn't it possible that in time, and with practice, he'll improve? And if he really is goofing up only to get you to take the job back, aren't you doing just what he expects by being so critical?"

Their view was that, given the equipment they had to

work with—namely the men they lived with—the situation was truly hopeless. They figured they'd get faster results waiting for a cheap vacuuming robot to go on the market.

Maybe they are right. Still, the more I heard, the more convinced I became that women may be either (1) doing the men an injustice by being so suspicious or (2) playing into their sneaky hands by being too impatient.

Let's take a closer look at the most common complaints:

*He is only pretending
he can't do it.*

Maybe. But this can also be a case of giving him too much credit and yourself too little. Just because a woman finds certain tasks, which she has done since childhood, to be a snap does not mean a man sees them the same way. I hate people who tell me "Any fool can do that" when it is perfectly plain to me that I can't. I also hate "It's so easy to put that together; a child can do it." And "This should take you no more than five minutes to run through." Some of us get very nervous when confronted with the unfamiliar.

In general, men have had very little exposure to household chores and may very well feel intimidated by them. I feel that when a man claims to be incompetent, he deserves the benefit of the doubt. Maybe he *is* incompetent.

One problem in getting women to believe this, of course, is the fact that, although we have all heard about the men who do nothing, we also keep hearing about the men who do everything. Veritable paragons of modern masculinity, they slice, they dice, they mince, they rinse, they chop, they mop, they sweep up and make beds. Beautifully, too.

I have a neighbor who claims that her husband notices when the cupboards need new shelf paper. Rather than merely commenting, "That paper looks kind of old, doesn't it?" he relines the shelves himself. His wife is quite smug about it.

We keep hearing about men who are wildly enthusiastic about their new role. Marci's husband Brian took over the cooking because Marci gets home from work much later than he. He discovered he loves cooking, and the meals he makes are dazzling. Much more so than Marci's. She can cook but doesn't like to. In fact, she admits her favorite recipe was "Open can, pour in pan, heat, eat."

However, just because these fellows exist does not mean that men who do not perform as well are to be despised. After all, a lot of people play the violin, but they all can't be Isaac Stern.

He always does it
the wrong way.

Who says it's the wrong way? On the one hand, a woman will say he should do half the work. On the other hand, she'll say the work should be done her way. She'll insist he put away the dishes, and then she'll get mad because he has picked a new place for the mixing bowl. Well, obviously, if she does the cooking, she has to be able to find the bowl. But there are two crucial questions here: is the bowl always in the *same* wrong place? Is that wrong place reachable? If the answers are yes, why not declare a new right place and let it go at that? (If he is playing a game of hide-the-bowl, however, your worst suspicions may be correct.)

For most of us, the right way is the way we have always done it, which probably means the way our mothers did it. But is that way the only way? One of my favorite stories is about a daughter who asks her mother why she always cuts off the end of the ham before baking it. Her mother says, "That's the way it's supposed to be done. My mother always did that." The daughter then asks her grandmother why this was necessary. And the grandmother replies that, in her case, it was necessary because she didn't have a baking pan big enough to hold a whole ham.

Who is to say that a fresh outlook might not reveal a better way or an equally good one? I once read an article by a man who took over his house and six children while his old style wife was in the hospital. He described how, instead of trying to get the whole house clean at once, he did one room or one task a day before leaving for work. He hardly noticed he was doing it, he said. I followed his system for years.

Sometimes this one gets down to a question of how flexible the woman is. Sometimes it gets down to: Can she accept the way *his* mother did it?

He does a terrible job.

The question that must be asked here is, Who gets to set the standards? If you are going to negotiate the decision as to who does the chores, you will probably have to negotiate the standards, too. How neat is neat? How clean is clean?

How important is doing it now versus doing it later? Sometimes the best thing for both sides is simply to lower the official mess threshold. Sometimes one is faced with renegotiating the chores.

In my house, if I care *very* much, I do it myself. Bernie's idea of a made bed is that all blankets should be present and accounted for. I can't stand a rumpled bed, so I make it. No negotiation necessary.

He refuses to learn.

Possibly. If he continually breaks dishes and burns roasts and shrinks sweaters, this can be very discouraging.

But first, have you been a patient teacher? Men complain that women make them feel stupid. As in "No, you don't cut it in chunks, you cut it in small pieces. Oh, here, let me do it." Or "Noooooo, you'll break them that way. Aaaaiiiiii! You have broken them. Get out of the way. Let me do it." This can lead to a certain lack of motivation.

There is also the possibility that you are asking him to learn the wrong things. A good manager tries to fit the right person to the right job. Bernie always tells me that. Someone who hates meeting people, for example, should not be a talk show host.

Let's say you are dealing with a macho male who would rather die than dust, one who would be humiliated if any of his friends saw him do housework. The right assignment for him, then, has to be tougher than flipping a feather duster, and it should be something that can be done inside and out of sight.

Let's say, further, you have persuaded him to vacuum,

on the premise that a vacuum is a machine and men are comfortable with machines. But he does not do corners. Analyze this job more carefully. The reason corners are difficult is that you have to move the furniture out of the way to get to them. But macho men are usually willing to move furniture. They pride themselves on being able to leap tall sofas with a single bound. Possibly you can work out an arrangement whereby he moves the furniture, you sweep the corners, and you are both finished in half the time. He never learns how to vacuum, but you no longer care.

He does it, but grudgingly.

If he does it, he does it. There is no law that says we have to enjoy everything we do. I put this one in the same category as the complaint that he insists on saying he is helping me when he is really helping himself. Picky, picky, picky. According to old style values, he is helping you.

He doesn't do anything, period.

Even this one bears closer inspection. If he doesn't do anything, does he still insist that you do everything? This makes a big difference. A woman I know says her husband doesn't expect her to do anything he wouldn't do and as result their house is a mess.

I know many houses that are definitely messier than they used to be. Women who used to iron every article of permanent press underwear are now willing to take the manufacturer's word for it. Women who used to scrub the kitchen floor every day have lowered their standards without noticeably affecting the family's health. There is more than one way to make life easier.

Also, does he take care of any of his own things? Does he feed *his* goldfish? Sometimes a man will sweep the cellar but not the living room, polish a gun collection but not the silver, wash a car but not a pair of pajamas, go to the cleaners but not the supermarket. I feel Bernie sends me the message I most want to hear just by taking his own shirts to the laundry and picking them up, too.

I know he does that, not because he thinks I do a bad job of ironing, but because he wants me to know that he knows I'm not totally responsible for his well-being. I still iron *my* shirts, but that's my choice. Bernie would rather pay than learn to iron; I would rather iron than have to pay. To each his or her own. I figure if a guy does anything, he deserves a little credit.

But he definitely does not get credit if he creates a mess and expects you to clean it up. This, however, is usually less a matter of getting him to do something than of convincing yourself not to do something. If you don't want to pick up his socks, stop. Nicely, but firmly. Now, it's his problem. Just be careful you don't trip over them.

Have you been specific about what you have asked him to do? Some women who claim their men do nothing have admitted to being very vague about what they wanted of them. They say, "I need some help around here. Do something." This is like saying, "Say something clever!" The usual response is "Huh?" As with anything else in life, there is an advantage in being prepared. A very specific request has more clout than a general one. As in "I have a big problem. Here is what I think you could do to help. If that doesn't suit, here is a possible alternative." Sometimes you have to give a man a way to respond favorably.

There are, of course, some very tough cases. One of my newspaper colleagues claims that men are congenitally unable to pick up after themselves. He is fond of quoting Mark Twain: "Have a place for everything and put it someplace else." He takes a macho pride in the fact that he can never find anything on his desk, buried as it is under tons of paper. If a man really wants to live that way, there is nothing anyone can do. But even here, one might succeed by starting with something relatively small. Say he gets home before you do. Maybe he would turn the burner on under the dinner you cooked that morning. If he won't even do that, a bread and water diet might help.

He does nothing but complain that I don't do enough.

This is truly the worst case of all. But even here there may be something to do before calling your lawyer. If he says the place is a mess, you might ask him just what must be done to solve that. If he mentions only one thing (the carpet is dusty), you might be willing to do just that—and still forget everything else. Or that might be a good time to suggest he take on the carpet while you do everything else.

Another system for resolving the conflict between his determination to do nothing and your determination to stop doing everything is to hire a third party to do something.

But if indeed all is lost, think about his other qualities. Surely, he has some. Why else would you love him? You

TWO CAN SWEEP AS NEATLY AS ONE

have to tolerate a certain amount of failure in him, just as he must tolerate it in you. My friend Nancy says she has tried for twenty years to get her husband not to leave his smelly pipe on the bathroom sink, but to no avail. Clearly somewhere in this man's early life he was frightened by a bathroom sink and feels that only a smelly pipe can protect him from it. We all have our weird ways.

Our society has its weird ways, too, and those weird ways operate against us in this realm. Even if a man is willing to take the kids to school, he may find that *his* boss is much less forgiving than *her* boss would be if the kids make him late. It's wrong, but it's there.

But the good news is that it is becoming increasingly common for men to take on so-called women's work. And that, in turn, makes it more acceptable. The word is even getting around that men's failure to cope with homey chores may shorten their lives. Yes. Research has discovered that widowers have a much higher mortality rate than widows— a much higher rate than can be explained by the normal tendency of women to live longer than men. And one obvious conclusion is that a woman left alone can still find her way to the store, the refrigerator, and the stove, but many men cannot.

Poor men. All their lives their food simply appeared on the table, their floors were swept, their dishes were washed and stacked away. And when they were left alone, they were bereft of more than love and affection; they lost the means to cope with the details of life. Where is the sugar? How much detergent does one use? It turns out that when long ago they'd said, "I'd die without you, my love," they were righter than they knew.

Men are moving into this arena slowly, to be sure, but they *are* moving. Sociologist John Scanzoni studied which chores men were most and least willing to assume. First came child care, then food shopping, then clothes washing, cooking, and dishwashing (buy a dishwasher). Cleaning is last on the list. Researchers on this subject have found that, if asked, men say they are willing to do more. Some would be happy to ask their mates to do less.

So, have hope. Think positively. Take the trouble to work with him. And remember to praise all efforts—either because that will encourage him to do the job better or because it will discourage him from thinking he can toss the whole mess back to you.

11

WORKING IT OUT

If I had to pick the single greatest influence on the relationship between men and women today, I wouldn't choose the pill, although that's close, and I wouldn't select all the laws that affect the rights of one or the other. I'd say it was the change in women's attitude about going out of the house to work.

I'm not claiming that merely having a job creates a new style woman because I know that's not so. After all, there are women who work but don't want to. There are women who are angry at their men for not supporting them as they believe it is a man's duty to do. There are women for whom working makes not the slightest bit of difference. I know a very successful businesswoman who, in her own home, is more traditional than my grandmother. And that's how she wants it, too. She waits on her husband hand and foot, and whatever he says goes.

But then, there are the rest of us, for whom having a job, an identity—and money—of our own has affected the way in which we see ourselves and the way we see the male-female relationship. Some sixty years ago, novelist Virginia Woolf noted that only after she inherited "500 pounds a year forever" from the estate of an aunt did she give up her "bitterness and anger toward men." (Virginia was quintessential new style.)

This is something, of course, that affects the majority of women. Some 52 percent of all women above age eighteen are employed and, as pollster Daniel Yankelovich discovered, half of all current full-time homemakers plan to be employed at some time. And not surprisingly, women tend to work* because they want to. A 1980 newspaper industry survey asked working women—and not just the hot-shot career types—whether they would choose to stay home if they could be guaranteed the same amount of money they were now earning, and three out of five said no thanks.

I admit I am biased on the subject of working. I have always earned money of my own and had a separate career of my own. Naturally, that effects my outlook. I'm convinced that my sense of independence is what enables me to love more completely. I'm with Bernie because I want to be, not because I have to be. And I think he enjoys knowing that, too.

Time and again when I talk to friends and acquaintances about what kinds of things have had a positive effect on their relationship, they don't much mention magic potions or incantations or threats at the point of gun. Maybe they don't want to tell me *everything*, but they often mention working.

"When we were first married," said Lynne, "I was more

---

*I hope everyone understands that when I say "working" I mean being employed outside the home only because that's a commonly understood word, and not because I think women who stay home to raise a family don't work.

traditional than he was. If he came into the kitchen to help me, I threw him out. But since I've been working, I welcome his help, and we really enjoy being together."

"He thinks that money is important and that the one who earns it is entitled to make the decisions," said Bonnie. "Well, the closer I came to becoming an accountant, the more he began to help me and consult with me. He just sees me differently, that's all."

"It seems to me that all the years I was home raising children," said Ellie, "I was angry at Ed. He seemed to control so much more than I did. All I had to control was the house and so, if he so much as moved a cup out of place, we had a fight. Now that I'm working, I'm not angry anymore. And I don't care where the cups are."

"Since I've been working, I don't argue with Dan about money every time the washer breaks down," said Rita. "I take care of having it fixed myself."

"Irv's a changed man since I started working," said Connie. "It used to be that the most important thing in his life was having a full-course dinner at the same time every night. But now he realizes I can't always do that, and so now we do all kinds of different things at dinnertime, not all of them having to do with eating, either. I also don't iron his socks anymore, and he has adjusted."

Every situation is different.

In Lynne's case, she had to change her attitude more than he did. This wasn't a case of *getting* him to help, but of *letting* him help.

Bonnie's guy didn't really change. But his attitude about money and power going together worked in her favor.

Ellie's Ed didn't change, either. But once she had

other things on her mind, she was too busy to be mad at him. There's something to be said for that.

Obviously, the fact that Rita can now get the washer fixed herself doesn't make Dan a new style husband. Still, to the extent that she makes some economic decisions and he doesn't care, she is just a bit more new style, and he is, too.

And Connie has discovered what nature has known since the world began—that when environments change, most species adapt. Obviously, some find they enjoy it more than others. What else would you expect? But woman's revolution is leading to man's evolution, and that's all there is to that.

A few years ago, Canadian researchers Ronald Burke and Tamara Weir interviewed both men and women for a study of "marital satisfaction and wives' employment." They interviewed couples in which the husbands were all professionals (engineers, accountants, etc.) and in which some of the wives worked (at a greater variety of jobs) but most did not.

They concluded from the various responses that the employed wives were in better psychological shape than the full-time homemakers and in better physical shape, too. Even though the employed women griped about having to do double work, even though they expressed anxiety and guilt about not fulfilling their traditional roles and taking proper care of their children, they were much happier than the nonanxious, nonguilt-ridden, "single work" homemakers.

And one clue as to why this might be was that the employed wives were more likely to report that disagreements with their husbands were resolved by "mutual give-and-take rather than giving in."

And what about the husbands? Did those with job-holding wives report themselves happier, too? As a matter of fact, they did not. The men with working wives complained of losing their support system. They felt the loss of that person who was always there when she was needed. Some felt they lost status by doing housework. They grumbled about having to go along with what their wives wanted when they didn't want to. Yet they said they did go along, either because they wanted "to see her happy" or because they were "resigned to the inevitable."

And here comes the really interesting part: even while reciting their woes, these husbands of employed wives reported greater communication and more areas of agreement with their wives than did the husbands of homemaking wives.

What are we supposed to make of that? In exchange for feeling guilty, she's happy. In exchange for losing support, he's gained closeness. Is that bad? Possibly she is not as guilt-ridden nor he as unhappy as each claims. Possibly they only think they *should* feel that way, and we may need another century to sort this out properly.

Sociologist John Scanzoni's studies on family decision-making showed beyond doubt that working wives are much more likely to have egalitarian relationships. Women derive both self-esteem and money from working, he says, and when it comes to mutual give and take, the closer two partners are in income, the greater her clout in negotiation, the closer they are in self-esteem, the greater her impact, too. This last, self-esteem, has a great deal of bearing on the lives of women I know who have left work to raise families. They no longer earn the money, but the knowledge that they did and could again seems to bolster their self-esteem.

Some twenty years ago, I read an article that had nothing to do with working women, but a lot to do with self-esteem, and it is one of those articles whose message has engraved itself on my brain. As best I can remember it was entitled "The Belle of the Ball Is the Girl Who Thinks She Is the Belle of the Ball."

It seems some university researchers wanted to see if they could turn a shy wallflower into a, well, belle of the ball. They secretly paid some star athletes and other big men on campus to ask an unpopular and unsuspecting young woman out. And, just as the researchers had hoped, all this attention imbued the wallflower with so much self-confidence and self-esteem that long after the experiment was over she was still popular. Nobody had to be paid to take her out.

Because she thought of herself as "somebody," the guys thought of her that way, too.

A lot of questions could be asked about this story, of course. Such as, what would happen to the poor girl's psyche if she ever found out her original suitors were paid? Or, was a government grant paying for this? Or, where were these researchers when *I* needed them? But I don't question the point of the story, which is that once you change your own behavior, it changes that of others around you.

I believe that my work—and the money I earn from it—is what gives me that inner conviction that a woman's role in marriage is not just to serve but to share, that a man's is not merely to command but to collaborate. Inner convictions lead to outer behavior to which others (unless they are dinosaurs) just naturally adapt. (A little, anyway.)

New York marketing expert Judith Langer did a study on working women and was struck by how many very busy women mentioned having "supportive husbands." That made her wonder which came first—the work commitment or male supportiveness? Not being chicken, she decided firmly on the former. It was true, she says, that some of the women said their relationship enabled them to give their energy to work, but she felt it more likely that the women were very determined in their goals and that their men recognized that and, in fact, were attracted by it.

You might ask, if a full-time homemaker values what she does—as she should—can't she be equally new style and achieve that same give-and-take? Of course. But history shows that it's harder. And that, no doubt, is why women have resorted in the past to trickier methods.

A woman I know owns a secondhand clothing store. The nicest things in her shop, she says, are not secondhand at all. They are brought in brand-new by two women whose wealthy husbands give them charge accounts but not cash. What these women do is charge a half-dozen dresses at a department store, take three home, and leave three at the secondhand shop for resale. They end up with only a fraction of what the dresses will cost their husbands, but it's in cash. Obviously, even though these women are getting around their unobservant husbands, and even though they live more lavishly than I, they have no give-and-take at all.

To be fair to men, it should be said that the change in women's attitudes about going out to work has come about so recently that it's really hard for men to know just what to think about it.

On one hand, there is more money, and so they buy things they could never afford before; on the other hand, the house becomes sloppier and she wants him to mop.

On one hand, he's proud of her and even brags about her at parties; on the other hand, he doesn't like it that their vacation plans had to be postponed because of her job. Bernie is very enthusiastic about my being a new style woman until he goes on an all-expenses-paid business trip to Someplace Swell and discovers I can't just take off and go along.

On one hand, he's happy that she seems content; on the other hand, he misses the way she used to cater to his every need.

On one hand, he is relieved that she is self-sufficient, because that takes a lot of pressure off him; on the other hand, he is upset at her independence because he feels less needed.

How an individual male responds to this change depends on whether he focuses on the positive or the negative. A guy might decide his ego is so out of joint that he deliberately tries to undermine the woman—by picking a fight just before she goes to work, for example. But others are quick to see advantages. For example, management professor Marta Mooney talked to husbands from both one-paycheck and two-paycheck families and found that the latter felt less pressured, more able to take risks, more able to start something new even though it might mean a lowered income for a while, or to survive a layoff, or to take an earlier retirement or a longer vacation. One-third of the two-paycheck husbands said they were considering a job change, while only 10 percent of the one-paycheck husbands said the same.

As Charles Lamb once said (I got this quotation along with a set of mixing bowls), "The good things in life are not to be had singly but come to us with a mixture."

This is true for men and for women, too. The good things that come with working bring along their own seasoning of annoyances. I am never home when anything is delivered. I am never home when the repair person comes. In addition to worrying about the equipment that breaks at home, like the heater that goes out when the blizzard is predicted, I can now worry about the equipment that breaks down at the office. Isn't that exciting?

Tensions are created that I know wouldn't exist if my time were totally my own (and his own), but other tensions would be there.

The trend is clearly in the direction of change for both men and women. I know there is a lot of hand wringing about this. U.S. Department of Labor statistics do show that employed wives have a greater propensity to divorce. That scares some women into feeling that if they become independent their husbands will leave them. But it is just as likely, if not more so, that those figures reflect wives whose new independence and income have allowed them to leave their husbands. We have no way of knowing whether in the long run that's good or bad. A National Research Council panel attempted to study the consequences of a working mother on children and concluded, as its chairman Dr. Sheila Kammerman put it, "You can no more universalize the consequences of a mother working than you can the consequences of the industrial revolution."

In his book, *New Rules*, Daniel Yankelovich reported that in 1938 when Americans were asked, "Do you disapprove of a married woman earning money even though her husband can afford to support her," 75 percent said yes. But in 1978, only 26 percent said yes. I suspect that if the public were quizzed about the industrial revolution before and after, the results would be about the same. We adjust.

Little by little, society is changing to accommodate a new reality. More convenience foods, stores open later, messier houses. Where once we had only the kind of advertisement in which Mrs. Olsen had to come to the rescue of a poor wife whose husband was about to leave her because she made such lousy coffee, we now see her after she gets her pilot's license, and he lovingly makes coffee for *her*. It's good, too.

Sigh.

12

GETTING A SECOND OPINION

I am a great believer in the value of a second opinion, and not just when the doctor claims your head will have to come off.

I have found that one of the problems of pairing off two by two is that sometimes when you put things to a vote, you end up with a one-to-one tie. Worse yet, he may claim his vote counts two and yours zip, or just as bad, neither one of you seems to know what to do. This is also a good time for a second opinion.

There are, of course, the obvious choices—the host of therapists, doctors, counselors, and gurus. But there are lots of other very useful, if less high-powered, resources—friends and family, acquaintances, and strangers.

Let me give you an example. One time Bernie and I could not agree on whether to build something on a lot we own next to our house, and if so, what. I suppose if he were totally old style he'd make the decision without me, but he's not. (Well, he had made a decision, of course, but he wanted me to agree with him.) If I were totally old style, I would agree with any decision he made, but I'm not.

For us this is the stickiest kind of question because he is a risk taker and I am not. He thinks it's fine to take a flyer. I want to hide our pennies under a rock.

And so we fought. Normally we believe in compromise and negotiation, but some decisions are yes or no, on or off, black or white; no compromise is possible. We often agree then that this time we'll do it his way and the next time mine, but that's only when neither of us is ready to die for his or her position.

We had been hassling over this for weeks, debating in our usual mature manner—he yells and I cry—but so far all we'd gotten out of it was a good case of the sulks. It was time to bring in a second opinion.

Bernie suggested we solve this through arbitration. If we could not agree on the plan itself, could we agree on one person whose opinion both of us respected and let that person decide for us?

Bernie is used to this idea because arbitration is common in solving disputes between management and labor. And in that world, there is a cadre of professional arbitrators to choose from. We didn't plan to be quite that formal. We would come up with an amateur arbitrator of our own.

What fun. We ran through names. There were lots of people whose opinions we respected, but there was the question of whether they might be biased in Bernie's or my direction. That eliminated his sisters and my brother, and portions of several other couples we knew. He thought the woman might side with me; I thought the man would be equally partial to him.

Finally, we did think of a name. This was a man we knew only casually, but we agreed that we respected his opinion and that he knew something about real estate. Bernie called him and asked if he'd like to save a marriage. He agreed. Bernie even offered to pay for his time, but he declined.

We ran this decision past him, and (the rat!) he sided with Bernie. But he also gave us some ideas neither one of us had thought of, so I felt better.

Actually, once I had agreed to the arbitration, I felt better anyway. At that point I knew there was at least a chance that I'd get my way, and even if I didn't (as it worked out), I wouldn't be left with the feeling I had been run over by a truck. If this venture doesn't work out eventually, I know there will be no hard feelings because we feel we have agreed to agree. We compromised in the only way we could—by getting a second opinion.

I suppose most of us do this in more casual ways. You can't agree whether the red chair looks good next to the blue wallpaper, so you ask your next-door neighbor who, you both agree, has good taste. You are in a twit over the proper hour for a kid's curfew so you canvass your friends to see what they do.

Whether casual or formal, the second opinion is a sensible alternative to the tantrums, oppression, crankiness, divorce, moping, mayhem, and melancholia that abound today. Some complications call for experts; some do not. Some people think they are programmed at birth with total lifetime instructions, but when the time comes to use them, the instructions usually turn out to be wrong. I think the best advice that can be given anyone is to feel free to seek advice.

Personally, I rather enjoy searching out second opinions. In fact, I can't resist learning about how someone solved a problem even when I don't have the problem ("Keeping romance alive while raising penguins in Antarctica"), or even when I suspect a solution may be worse than the problem ("How I learned to live with cockroaches by turning them into pets").

I find that sometimes the simplest suggestion will have a lot of merit ("Take the first parking space you see; there won't be one closer to the store"). And you never know when a seemingly offhand remark will have a major impact on your life. Psychologist Carl Rogers claimed that was the case with a single sentence said to him by a professor when he was a student: "Don't be an ammunition wagon; be a rifle." You just never know what is going to catch on.

Advice, I think, is somewhat like fashion. Either it is your style or it isn't. It works for you or it doesn't. You are comfortable with it or you are not. I have interviewed countless advice-givers, some learned, some not, some expensive, some for free, and many of them believe they have discovered a code of life in one-size-fits-all. I haven't found it works that way.

I remember one fellow who wrote a book on creative sex. He insisted that the path to ecstasy for everyone was to have intercourse in a hammock suspended from the bedroom ceiling. He wrote of falling in love, but I envisioned falling in plaster. Whatever turns you off, as they say.

And then there was a book, published a few years ago, called *Juggling: The Art of Balancing Marriage, Motherhood, and Career*. The author, Letitia Baldrige, was indisputably involved in all three. For one thing, she was president of her own public relations firm.

GETTING A SECOND OPINION

Tish's system for handling the home-job hassle included a full-time "live-in, Irish-born, British-trained nannie" to look after the kids. This gives a working mother "peace of mind," she said. A live-in nannie is much to be preferred over a succession of baby-sitters, she advised. Who would argue with that?

The nannie could not be expected to do housework as well as look after children, of course. Tish said she solved that problem by employing a three-days-a-week housekeeper, plus a seamstress and a laundryman. There was also a doorman at her New York apartment building who was always available to accept deliveries or let the plumber in if, for some reason, the nannie, housekeeper, seamstress, laundryman, or Tish did not happen to be around.

The working mother, Tish went on to advise, should not neglect herself even while caring for her family. She herself, she reported, always made sure to keep regular appointments at her beauty parlor and to get weekly massages from Miraculous Max, her masseur. Get-away-from-it-all weekends also help, she said.

Would the Baldrige blueprint make the juggle less of a struggle? I believed it. Did I ever. I just couldn't afford it. For me, getting advice on balancing home and career from Letitia Baldrige was like getting advice on my weekly food budget from David Rockefeller or J. Paul Getty. "Caviar is a good buy. Check out the truffles."

Some people say that you should seek advice only from those who are willing to follow it themselves. I don't share that bias. I'm sure Letitia did just as she told us, but that didn't make her advice helpful to me. On the other hand,

I know a marriage counselor who is truly a wonder at helping others—even though none of his four ex-wives has anything good to say about him.

Obviously, some people would be better off if they practiced what they preached. You may recall the recent, much-publicized case of Michael Morgenstern, who wrote the best-seller *How to Make Love to a Woman*. He advised men against a "macho attitude," which sounds very sensible to me. The fact that he didn't follow his own advice—and punched a young woman—did not lessen its value. Indeed, I thought that the fact that the young woman sued and collected only reinforced his point.

I concede it's disconcerting to discover that someone who is giving advice isn't living it. Marabel Morgan, author of *The Total Woman* and one of the best-known advice-givers of our time, comes to mind. You may remember Marabel for her suggestion that one can put zip into a romantic relationship by showing up at the door at dinnertime dressed only in baby-doll pajamas or Saran Wrap. Presumably, the man at the door was to be one's husband, not some wandering stranger looking for directions.

But that wasn't really the heart of Marabel's message. A dozen years ago, she recognized that many women were feeling unsatisfied and unappreciated in marriage and wanted to know what to do about it. Her answer was simply to turn the clock back.

The way to happiness, advised Marabel, was to become an old style woman—to accept the idea that whenever husband and wife disagree, he wins. A woman should always adapt to the man's way of doing things, Marabel said, and if she tells herself she is doing it voluntarily, she will no longer feel resentful.

Did Marabel really believe that? Maybe so. Did Marabel *do* that? According to her second book, *Total Joy,* she didn't have to. Marabel reported that, fortunately for her, she rarely had to adapt to *her* man's way of doing things: "Charlie and I work out most of our conflicts at the compromise level."

One just has to be a little more careful about advice from those who want you to do as they say but not as they do. Sometimes such advice-mongers are thinking more of themselves than of you. When I was writing a book about divorce, a lawyer told me, "I could settle cases much faster if friends didn't keep putting their two cents in. It seems there is always a best friend at my client's elbow urging her to get the S.O.B. or urging her not to let him get away with any crap! They're the people who'd really like to sock it to their own mates, but they don't have the guts. So they live vicariously through the fights of others."

Sometimes the best kind of second opinion is not, strictly speaking, advice. It's the service a friend does you by just listening when you want to talk. It's the simple retelling of their own story that makes you feel more comfortable about what's happening to you.

My friend Julie says that when she and John, newly married, erupted into argument, she was sure their love was gone. Heartsick, she confided in her mother, who said, "You call that a fight? That's nothing. Daddy and I had bigger fights than that." Remarked Julie, "They must have had them after the children were sleeping or two miles out of sight. I don't remember my parents ever raising their voices, but I can tell you I was very relieved to hear about it."

Sometimes the source of a second opinion doesn't even have to be human. I know a couple who claim that whenever the pressure is on in their house, they seek help from a family friend named Pee Dee, who happens to be a stuffed frog.

They had never planned to turn this frog into a therapist. Who ever heard of a Freudian frog? It just worked out that way.

They'd bought the frog in a gift shop near the Pee Dee River in South Carolina, which explains the name, plunked him on a shelf at home, and that was that. But then one day, one of the boys did something that made his mother so angry she didn't want to listen to his excuses. She didn't want to listen to anything he had to say. So he turned to Pee Dee and he said, "Pee Dee, would you talk to Mom for me? Please tell her I'm sorry." That broke the ice and started a family tradition.

Thereafter, whenever anyone in the family seemed unapproachable, Pee Dee was asked to be the carrier of messages, the bringer of apologies. He would show up on pillows with little notes of explanation. It was hard to sulk for long when Pee Dee got involved. On the other hand, you didn't have to read the notes right away if you didn't feel like it. Pee Dee would wait. Pee Dee always got everybody talking again. When Pee Dee's advice was sought, it was always done loudly, so that the rest of the family would know somebody thought advice was needed.

GETTING A SECOND OPINION

To show their appreciation for all Pee Dee did for them, the family always remembered to give him gifts at Christmas. When they went on vacations, they sent him postcards. Pee Dee went to college with one of the daughters and for years afterwards her friends sent him letters. He went along to one son's senior prom. When one of the daughters got married in Texas, Pee Dee went to the wedding—in his own tuxedo. He shows up, a little green about the gills and proud of it, all over the family photograph album.

If I thought this would work for everyone, I wouldn't just write about it, I'd rush out and open a frog factory. Of course, if I opened a frog factory, some psychiatrist would write a learned paper to the effect that frogs are fine, but bunnies are better. And then where would I be?

The point is, there is an infinite variety of second opinions available. Sometimes you needn't say a thing but just watch somebody who seems to be doing things right. A couple of years ago, I wrote a newspaper story about two sisters who did just that. This pair had written a book, *Sidetracked Household Executives*, about how to clean your house.

The sisters claimed that they had once been terrible slobs. Their houses were always dirty. They had greasy dishes in the sink. There was peanut butter on their cabinet handles. Ychhhh. On top of that their checkbooks were overdrawn.

Their spouses were unhappy about this. In fact, one sister's marriage broke up, and the other's was on the brink. They were desperate to clean up their acts, which meant cleaning up their rooms. So they turned to a friend whose house was always neat and asked her if they could watch for a while to see how she managed it.

The sisters discovered that whenever this friend opened a drawer, she closed it again. When something fell, she picked it up. When she finished using a tea bag, she threw it away instead of just tossing it into the sink. She seemed, well, organized! The sisters reacted as if they had discovered penicillin. They decided they would get organized, too.

But what seemed to come easily to their friend did not come easily to them. The solution was right, but they had to develop a method of their own, which they did. First they listed every single chore to be done in a house: wipe faucet, dust top of table, bathe dog. They wrote these on separate file cards and arranged them according to daily, weekly, and even yearly duties. They scheduled them in order of importance. And then they began to do them one by one. Pretty soon their houses were so clean, they said, you could do open-heart surgery on the floor.

My first reaction to this was astonishment. They can't remember to empty a dishwasher unless they check a file card first? They have to *practice* closing drawers? They have to consult a list to find out what to do in the morning?

But the more I thought about it, the more I realized these sisters were on to something. Unlike their friend, they viewed housekeeping as a problem too big to get hold of. They wanted to do something about it but didn't know where to start. By writing down every chore and specifying a time to do it, they broke down the formidable whole into doable units. Just because their particular goal was a non-

gummy door handle didn't make their solution less profound.

I learned that same lesson myself years ago. I was supposed to be writing a book, and not a single word came out. I was really in a funk about it, since I'm supposed to be a professional writer. Well, I consulted a writer friend for—what else?—advice, and she said my trouble was that I was thinking of writing a *whole book* and that thought was paralyzing me. I should think instead of writing just one chapter, after which, I would maybe write another. And possibly, another after that. Worked like a charm.

It seems to me that kind of advice should probably be coupled with any other advice you acquire. And that is, you can't do everything at once; you needn't think in terms of total change. Just pick a place and start it. Just because you can't think of a way to transform your guy *totally* doesn't mean you can't convince him to change a little, and then maybe a little more. If nothing happens, try something else.

All my years as an advice junkie have taught me that nothing works for everyone. But I wouldn't be writing all of this if I didn't believe that whatever seems to work for some is worth passing along.

13

THERE ARE LIMITS

The best and strongest bond between two people will still not protect either one from struggle, boredom, illness, worry, anger, disappointment, mistakes, and all the other things that make life so interesting. Even fairy princesses who live happily ever after get cavities. The most devoted mother has moments when she would stash the kids in a spaceship whether they wanted to see Mars or not. The most impassioned lover sometimes gets tired.

Not, of course, that we want to believe this. No, we want perfection.

In her book *The Second Sex*, Simone de Beauvoir complained bitterly about men wanting, well, everything. He wants her to be "at once warm and cool in bed... to be wholly his and yet no burden... to establish him in a fixed place on earth and to leave him free... to assume the monotonous daily round and not bore him... to be always at hand and never importunate. He wants her all to himself and not belong to her, to live as one of a couple and to remain alone."

A woman is betrayed from the very beginning, in de Beauvoir's opinion, because all the obligations are on her side, and they're impossible.

And, of course, women do resent this old style outlook. But as we set out to right this wrong, it appears we have come up with some tough standards of our own for men. He must be brave in the face of danger ("The bullet only went through my shoulder, ma'am; nothin' to fret about") but also warm and vulnerable. He must be protective, yet not overbearing. He must always be there when we need him, yet understand that we need time for ourselves. He should be good-looking, adventurous, and sexy, but also faithful and a good father. He should be successful and respected in the community, but spend most of his time with us. He should be cool and strong, yet hot and lively. He should be brilliant and creative but never bored when we are less so, or annoyed when we are more so. He should feel we are totally his equal and yet, if there is a noise downstairs at night, he should find out what it is. He should make a very nice living, but value our contribution. He must not only place his cloak in the mud so that we don't dirty our slippers, but thereafter take it to the cleaners himself.

All we desire is to live a stress-free life, tapping our potential to the maximum with dynamic results, supported by an adoring and adorable male. Is this too much to ask? Yes.

What we want, to be disgustingly realistic, is unobtainable. In love, as in everything else, we usually have to arrange our priorities. What do you want most? Where are you willing to compromise? What trade-offs can you make? How much of what is lacking really matters? In some areas of life it probably pays to aim for the top, dare to be great, reach for the stars, and not accept second best, but in love it's better to compromise. Maybe you won't get everything you want, but then, neither will he.

THERE ARE LIMITS

Nobody does. I don't care how many articles confront us about those couples who have everything, who are so incredibly close they seem cloned. I've read how she handles kids, career, and castle with effortless efficiency, while he is supportive, sensual, and extraordinarily rich. You could get the impression that everybody is living in absolute bliss except you and the Joneses down the street who throw pots and pans from the window.

But this is an illusion I don't live with. I write enough stories about the famous to realize they aren't telling all they know. I have written about couples who seem to be leading an enchanted existence—until the divorce papers are filed or the memoirs are written, until the scandal erupts or she is arrested after his body is found and her fingerprints are on the knife. "I'm really shocked," the next-door neighbor always says. "They seemed like such a loving couple."

I have nowhere told you that my Bernie is perfection, even though I have said that to him. Nor would I have the gall to claim that I am so easy to live with even though, when we are not disagreeing about something, that is what he tells me. Because I adore Bernie, I would willingly jump on the railroad tracks to save him; if somebody were shooting at him, I'd throw myself in the way. He can have the last life preserver, and I'll go down with the ship—but that doesn't mean I'd promise not to fight with him or always to take his advice. There are limits.

In some ways it is truly amazing that we get along as well as we do, considering our differences: he always wants to take a walk when I want to lie on the beach; he is generous while I am, uh, economical ("You gave them *how much?*"); he watches late movies on TV when I want to read; and where our daughter Carole is concerned he is an alarmist ("*What!* She bought a *motorcycle?*") while I stay calm.

I have claimed only that where there exists a common desire to remain together, you can take something that is basically good and make it even better. I have found that to be so. The secret of happiness, I have been told over and over by those who counsel the miserable, is to find that happy medium between believing nothing can change and therefore giving up and believing you can have everything and therefore never being satisfied with what you've got. I tend to endorse that theory, since I ricochet from one to the other often enough to know how to be miserable, but I end up in the middle often enough to keep my outlook bright.

All of which means I have my priorities. I'd rather have a supportive man than a fabulously rich one. Not that I'd get upset if Bernie became fabulously rich, you understand, I merely cite my priorities in order of importance.

Obviously, there are those who would take an opposite point of view. Humorist Harry Golden used to tell the tale of Mrs. Lipshitz who wore a diamond the size of an egg. A friend commented that Mrs. L. was certainly lucky to have such a fabulous jewel. "True," said Mrs. Lipshitz, "but of course, you realize that along with the Lipshitz Diamond comes the Lipshitz Curse."

"And what is that?" her friend asked of Mrs. Lipshitz.

"Mr. Lipshitz," came the reply.

I don't expect everyone to want what I want, though I admit I am sometimes amazed at others' choices. I once met a woman in a hospital emergency room whose husband had broken her arm and beaten her black and blue. I knew of a shelter for abused women, so I asked her if she wanted to leave him. She was indignant at the suggestion. "Leave my Billy? I'd die first," she said. And she probably will, because Billy will see to that. But what could I say?

Men can be equally mystifying. Just recently, a New Jersey jury convicted a wife of conspiring with her lover to murder her husband. The prosecutor produced letters she had written to her lover in which she called her mate El Jerko. But did any of the testimony lessen El Jerko's marital affection? It did not. He was in court every day to root for his wife, and he attacked the jury for "wrecking" his family.

Clearly there is no single recipe for romance. Not every woman wants what I call a new style relationship—a partnership with a man who is lover and friend, but not boss. All I'm trying to say in these pages to those, like me, who do, is that men *can* be moved in that direction.

Well, okay, maybe not *all* men. If he tends to murmur endearments like "Only one of us can wear the pants in this family" or "Who pays the bills around here anyhow" or "Have you met my ball and chain?" or, in true Archie Bunker tradition, "Stifle it, Edith," I'll grant you he's a tough case.

How close you can come to each other depends on how far you are apart. There is a scene in the movie *Annie Hall* in which the two halves of a couple, Annie and Alvy, are talking with their psychiatrists. The screen is split so that we see both of them at once. His shrink asks him, "Do you often sleep together?"

Alvy replies, "Hardly ever. Maybe three times a week."

Her shrink asks her, "Do you have sex often?"

Annie answers, "Constantly. Three times a week."

I'm sure we all recognize that the world of romance has its own equivalents to earthquakes, tornadoes, fires, and floods, where simple home remedies just don't apply. But most of us aren't dealing with earthquakes, just a little storm now and again. Most have a guy who's worth a try.

Some of the women I've talked to are annoyed at being told that *they* should take the initiative in improving their relationship and have accused me of being a closet old style woman for even suggesting it. They'll say, "Why is it always the *woman* who has to do or stop doing something? Why don't you write a book for men?"

Because they won't read it, that's why. In Shakespeare's *Henry IV, Part 2*, Glendower says, "I can call spirits from the vasty deep." And Hotspur replies, "Why, so can I or so can any man, but will they come when you do call for them?" In other words, my "calling" would be a waste of time. Because men are, by and large, not the ones complaining. And it is always the responsibility of the rebel, who wants to change the status quo, to make the first move. He who wants to keep things as they are need only do nothing.

If you want him to change, then you must act—by speaking up for what you want (if you haven't), by no longer nagging (if you have), by adopting more effective means of communication, and by refusing to be the same old you. Sooner or later the vasty deep will be heard from.

Some women feel guilty about pushing for change. This is a sticky issue because from time immemorial women have been accused of marrying men in order to change them. You know, "A woman doesn't want to marry a perfect man because then she'd have nothing to do." And men seem to know how to be righteous in their resistance: "That's how I am. You knew that when you married me."

Yet, I've said before and I'll repeat myself: if one partner is dissatisfied, change is inevitable. The only question is what kind of change? It's really a favor to both of you to work on change that will keep you comfortably together.

Everyone I talked to who claims she has, well, a newer kind of relationship says that even if her guy didn't want the changes she proposed, he went along once he realized it was very important to her.

I've admitted earlier that you really can't change a personality. If a man is not ambitious, he probably won't become so just because you say you'd like that. You can only ask for something another person has the power to give. You can't get diamonds from the Rhinestone Cowboy. A man can't sweep you away on a white charger if he doesn't have a horse. *He can't be somebody else.*

And society, although changing, isn't yet giving new style men the reinforcement they need. An attorney I know said that she worked when her husband went to school and then, when she got a chance to go to school in another state, he agreed to quit his job and find another in order to move there with her. "His parents just about collapsed at that," she reports. "The other men at his office (he is also an attorney) could not understand." Still, she and her husband did it, and both have survived nicely.

Many men are doing things now that their mothers

never imagined—and that they never imagined either. They are learning how to say, "What do you think about it?" They are taking care of the kids. They are compromising and admitting it. Quips my friend Robin, "That fellow who married me to keep me barefoot and pregnant is downstairs now making our dinner."

When we want to, we find resources we didn't know we had. I always think of a divorced guy I know who, when married, could not hear an alarm clock in the morning. His ex-wife claimed it took her ten minutes every day to shake him awake. She used to turn up the radio and wave a fragrantly steaming cup of coffee under his nose until, finally, his eyes would open. Now that they are parted, for reasons other than this, he has his own apartment. He also has an alarm clock with a pingy little ring as soft as a butterfly's flutter, and he has never overslept.

Some people really make changes that are volcanic. Barbara Pryor, whose husband is U.S. Senator from Arkansas, told the *Washington Post* that after years of protecting her husband from hassles, from the tire that's flat and the broken refrigerator, she announced to him one day that she was leaving. She was suffocating, she said. She had to go off and "find herself." It was, she said, a "tremendous shock to his system." I'll bet. But, she went on to say, they eventually got back together, on new terms, in a new way because "I like him so much and he likes me."

In all fairness, I have to say that most women to whom I talked mentioned compromise. Yes, he changed, but they accepted that some things would not change. Yes, he'll clean out the refrigerator, but she's still the one who knows when it has to be done. Yes, he'll now share decisions in more areas—but not in all.

"I know he didn't like the idea of my taking this job, because it keeps me away from home so often. But I make a point of not scheduling meetings two nights in a row, of making sure that I'm not out too many times a month so that I can be with him, and it's worked out fine."

"I know I'll never go as far in my career as I could if I didn't have a husband and children. But I want them, too, and so I've decided not to bid for certain assignments. I suppose some would say, Why doesn't he stay home with the kids for a few years? But neither of us wants that."

"I remind myself of what is important in my marriage. He isn't as enthusiastic about my career as I'd like, but it's nice to come home to someone who loves you. Sometimes, when he falls asleep on the couch and I am still raring to go, I say, how exciting is that? But then he kisses me in the morning, and I think I'm lucky he's there."

"I've divided my life into the musts and the shoulds, and I've discovered there aren't as many of the former as we both used to think. Maybe the house should be cleaner, but it doesn't have to be."

I found that most women with whom I talked about being a new style woman in love with an old style man would say, "That's me, all right." Yet many of them would add, "But my guy is better than most."

One might conclude that these women think most men are modeled after Dracula. I prefer to conclude only that more men are willing to make some kind of effort than is generally known.

You can moan that progress is glacial, but you can take some comfort in the knowledge that progress is possible. You might just as well be philosophical about it. I like to recall the comments of a woman I met who seemed to be one of the most new style types around. She said maybe that was so, but it hadn't been easy. "We respect each other," she said, "but we have also considered murder or divorce at least eight thousand times. We have moved closer. He has made an effort. I have made concessions. I figure you can only do so much in one lifetime, and it's only fair to leave something for the next generation to do."